D1460578

YOU
WILL
RECEIVE
POWER

YOU WILL RECEIVE POWER

WILLIAM LAW

Whitaker House

YOU WILL RECEIVE POWER

ISBN: 0-88368-476-4
Printed in the United States of America
Copyright © 1997 by Whitaker House

Whitaker House
30 Hunt Valley Circle
New Kensington, PA 15068

Library of Congress Cataloging-in-Publication Data

Law, William, 1686–1761.
    You will receive power / by William Law.
        p.   cm.
    ISBN 0-88368-476-4 (pbk.)
    1. Spiritual life—Christianity. 2. Holy Spirit. I. Title.
BV4501.2.L3585   1997
248.4—dc21   97–36560

1 2 3 4 5 6 7 8 9 10 11 12 / 06 05 04 03 02 01 00 99 98 97

Contents

Chapter 1

The Spirit
of True Religion

I can think of one thing that is a common concern among all Christians and that should be carefully examined by them. I am sure that if it were either neglected, overlooked, or mistaken by them, there would be some sad consequences. This is something that is essential to Christian salvation. I use the words *essential to salvation* because I would not turn my own thoughts, or call the attention of Christians, to anything but the one necessary and essential thing. It is only available as we rise out of our fallen state and become, as we were at our creation, the holy offspring of God and the real partakers of the divine nature.

What is this one thing? It is the renewal of the original life and power of the Spirit of God in us. Nothing else is needed by us, nothing else is intended for us, either by the Law, the Prophets, or the Gospel. Nothing else can make sinful man become a godly creature again. Everything else, no matter what it is—however glorious and divine in outward appearance—is dead and helpless unless it has the Spirit of God breathing and living in it. All

Scripture bears full witness to this truth. No angel, no person, no church, no reformation can do anything for us without the Spirit of God.

Everything written in the Bible was written only to call us back from the spirit of Satan, the flesh, and the world, to be again fully dependent upon and obedient to the Spirit of God. Out of love and thirst for our souls, the Holy Spirit seeks to have His original power of life in us. When this is done, all that the Scriptures can do for us is also done.

Read whatever doctrine of Scripture you will, and it will leave you as poor and empty and unreformed as it found you, unless it has turned you wholly and solely to the Spirit of God. Delight in whatever passage of Scripture you can find, and your delight will be nothing unless it has strengthened your union with and dependence upon Him. For when delight in matters of Scripture is a delight that is merely human, it is only the self-love of fallen man. It can have no better nature than this until it proceeds from the inspiration of God, awakening His own life and nature within us, which alone can bring forth a godly love in us.

Because it is an immutable truth that *"no man can say that Jesus is the Lord, but by the Holy Ghost"* (1 Cor. 12:3), it must be an equally immutable truth that no one can have a Christlike mind or the power of goodness unless he is led and governed by the Holy Spirit. Allow me to explain what I mean by this.

Goodness Is in God Alone

All possible goodness, whether named or nameless, was in God from all eternity. Therefore, for all

8

eternity it must be inseparable from Him; it can be nowhere but where God is. Before God created anything, there was only One who was good. Likewise, even after God created the innumerable hosts of blessed and holy and heavenly beings, there was and still is only One who is good, and He is God (Matt. 19:17).

All that can be called goodness, holiness, or heavenly inclinations in us is not our own, nor can it be considered the result of any of our own powers. Rather, all that is called divine goodness and virtue in us is nothing but the goodness of God manifesting itself according to how our created nature is able to receive it. This is the unalterable relationship between the Creator and the creature. Forever and ever, goodness can only belong to God. It is as essential to Him and inseparable from Him as His own unity.

God could not make the creature to be great and glorious in itself; this is as impossible as it would be for God to create beings who are not dependent upon Him. *"The heavens,"* said David, *"declare the glory of God"* (Ps. 19:1), and no creature can declare any other glory but that of God. If we wish to say that a divine or heavenly creature shows forth its own natural power, it might as well be said that the earth shows forth its own handiwork. (See Psalm 19:1.)

True Religion Depends upon God

However, all that is divine, great, and glorious in us is only a reflection of the greatness, glory, majesty, and blessedness of God dwelling in us and giving forth His own triune life, light, and love. As

9

much as we are able to receive these things, we may infallibly see the true ground and nature of all true faith, including when and how we may fulfill all our duties to God. Man's true religion is in rendering to God all that is God's, and in continually acknowledging that everything he is, has, and enjoys is from God.

This is the one true religion of all intelligent beings, whether in heaven or on earth, for they all have the same relationship to God. Although the various members of God's creation are different in many ways, the same standard of behavior toward God is required of them all. What is this one relationship that is the ground of all true religion and is the same between God and all intelligent creatures? It is a total and unalterable dependence upon God; it is continually receiving directly from God every kind and degree of goodness, blessing, and happiness that ever could be found.

The highest angel has nothing of its own that it can offer to God—no more light, love, purity, perfection, or glorious hallelujahs that spring from itself or its own powers, than the poorest creature upon earth. If this angel were to claim that a spark of wisdom, goodness, or excellence came from or belonged to itself, its place in heaven would be lost as surely as Lucifer lost his.

But the angels are ever abiding flames of pure love, always ascending up to and uniting with God, because the wisdom, power, glory, majesty, love, and goodness of God alone are all that they see and know. Songs of praise to their heavenly Father are their ravishing delight, because they know and feel that the breath and Spirit of their heavenly Father

sings and rejoices in them. Their adoration never
ceases because they never cease to acknowledge the
all of God—the entirety of God in the whole creation. This is the one religion of heaven, and nothing
else is the truth of religion on earth.

The Power and Presence of God

The matter is really very simple. The benefit
that we receive from faith is the power and presence
of God living and working in our beings. Because
this is the unchangeable blessedness that may be
gained from faith in God, we must receive all our
religious goodness wholly and solely from God's direct operation in our hearts. No one can possibly
have more of what is good and blessed in religion by
any use of his own natural powers. This is because
the creature cannot take God's blessings by its own
power any more after its creation than it could before it was created.

If truth forces us to believe that the natural
powers of created man could only come from the
power of God, the same truth should surely force us
to confess that we can only be comforted, enlightened, and blessed by the things in which God operates directly. Peace, joy, goodness, and rest can be
had in no other way, nor by any other thing, than in
and by God.

God's Creatures Seek Him

We often hear it said that religion does a glorious
work in the heart of man. But if the work is not begun, continued, and completed by the living operation

of God in man, it can have no truth, goodness, or divine blessing in it. Why? Because nothing can truly seek God except that which comes from God. Nothing can truly find God as its good except that which has the nature of God living in it. Therefore, we cannot perform any religious service with any truth, goodness, or blessing in it unless we do so by the divine nature that lives and breathes in us.

All true religion is, or brings forth, an essential union and communion of the spirit of the creature with the Spirit of the Creator. God in us, and we in God—one life, one light, one love. The Spirit of God first sows the seed of divine union in the soul of a man. Then, afterward, faith revives the seed, raises it up, and brings it forth to a fullness of life in God.

Allow me to illustrate this further. The beginning of life for an animal must first come from the breath of this world. As long as the animal is alive, it maintains an essential union with the breath of this world. In a similar manner, divine faith, hope, love, and willing submission to God are the breath of the religious life. As long as they are genuine, they unite God and the creature in the same living and essential manner as the breath of an animal unites it with the breath of this world.

Now, no animal could begin to breathe with the breath of this world unless its breath came from the air of this world. Likewise, no creature—whether angel or man—could begin to be religious or breathe forth faith, love, and a desire for God, unless a living seed of these divine virtues was first brought forth in him by the Spirit of God. Remember, a tree or plant can only grow and bear fruit by the same power that first gave birth to the seed. In the same way, faith, hope, and love for God can only grow and bear fruit by the power that first planted the seed of them in the soul.

The Holy Spirit plants the seeds of divine faith, hope, and love in the soul, but He also continually waters and cares for them. Such inspiration is vital to the continuance of a truly godly life. Therefore, divine inspiration is inseparable from true religion. If you were to take away inspiration, or if it were to cease, then no religious acts or feelings would give forth anything that is godly or divine. Created beings can offer nothing to God in return except what they have first received from Him. Therefore, if we are to offer to God all our divine inclinations and aspirations, we must have the divine and godly nature living and breathing in us.

Can anything reflect light before it has received light? Or can any other light be reflected than that which is received? Can any creature experience earthly emotions before it has an earthly nature? This is as likely as someone experiencing divine affections before partaking of the divine nature. It simply cannot be done!

Selfish and Vain Religion

A religious faith that is uninspired—a hope or love that does not proceed from the direct working of the divine nature within us—can do no more divine good to our souls and can no more unite them with the goodness of God, than a hunger after earthly food can feed us with the immortal Bread of Heaven. All that the natural or uninspired man does in the church has no more of the truth or power of divine worship in it than that which he does in the field or the shop through a desire for more money.

This is because all the acts of natural man, whether relating to matters of religion or to the world, are equally selfish, and there is no possibility of their being otherwise. Self-love, self-esteem, self-seeking, and living wholly to oneself are all that is or possibly can be in the natural man. Man cannot be any better, nor can he act any higher above this nature, than any beast. No creature can be in a better or higher state than this until something supernatural is found in it, and this supernatural something is called the Word or Spirit or Inspiration of God. This alone can give man the first good thought about God. The Holy Spirit of God is the only force that can cause man to have more heavenly desires than fleshly ones.

A religion that is not wholly built upon this supernatural ground, but instead stands solely upon the powers, reasonings, and conclusions of the natural, uninspired man, does not have even a hint of true religion in it. Instead, it is nothing, in the same sense that an idol is nothing because it has none of what it is alleged to have. Along the same lines, the work of religion has no divine good in it until it brings forth and keeps up an essential union of the spirit of man with the Spirit of God. This essential union cannot be formed unless there is love on both sides. More explicitly, it is not merely love, but it is love that has the same divine nature on both sides.

Love Brought to Us by the Spirit

No one, therefore, can reach God with his love or have union with Him by it besides the person who is inspired by the one Spirit of love—the Spirit with which God loved Himself from all eternity, before there were any created beings. Infinite hosts of newly created heavenly beings could not begin any new kind of love for God, nor could they begin to love Him at all if His own Holy Spirit of love had not been brought to life in them.

This love, with which God loved Himself from all eternity and which was then in God alone, is the only love in us that can draw us to God. We can have no power to cleave to Him, to will what He wills, or to adore the divine nature, except by partaking of that eternal Spirit of love.

Therefore, the continual, direct inspiration or operation of the Holy Spirit is the only possible ground for our continual love for God. Concerning this inspired love, and no other, John said, *"He that dwelleth in love dwelleth in God"* (1 John 4:16). If it were any other love, brought forth by any other thing but the Spirit of God breathing His own love in us, then John's words cannot be true. But we know that *"every word of God is pure"* (Prov. 30:5) and that His *"word is truth"* (John 17:17).

Chapter 2

The Inspiration
of the Spirit

D ivine inspiration was indeed essential to man's first created state. It is what I call man's first life source. The Spirit of the triune God, which breathed life into him, was the only force that made man a holy creature in the image and likeness of God. To have no other mover, to live under no other guide or leader but the Spirit, constituted all the holiness that the first man could have from God. If he had not been like this at the very beginning— God in him and he in God, brought into the world as a true offspring of the Holy Spirit—no dispensation, or revelation, would have directed fallen man to the Holy Spirit. I sometimes wonder if there would have been any mention of the Spirit's inspiration in man.

Fallen man cannot be directed to any good except the good he already had before he fell. If the Holy Spirit had not been man's first life source, no inspired prophets or holy men, speaking as they were moved by the Holy Spirit, would ever have been heard of. Such a thing would have been impossible! No fallen, sinful individual could have been inspired by the Holy Spirit unless the first life source of man was the true and real cause of such inspiration.

By the mercy and free grace of God, every fallen person has a secret remainder of divine inspiration preserved in him, though it is hidden, or rather, swallowed up by flesh and blood. This secret remainder was signified and assured to Adam by the name of a "bruiser of the Serpent," or "seed of the woman." (See Genesis 3:15.) This was Christ, who came to give the Holy Spirit, for the breath of the Spirit was the only way for mankind to be called and revived again into the divine life that he had before the Fall.

Consequently, it is clear that the gospel state is God's last dispensation and the finishing of man's redemption, because its whole work is a work of the Spirit of God in the spirit of man. All God's dispensations have been for the sake of that first godly and holy life that was born in the soul of the first man, Adam, and to which he died.

Direct and Continual Inspiration

But now, the gospel dispensation has come after all the Old Testament types and foreshadowings of redemption, to bring forth again in man a true and full birth of the Holy Spirit, as he had at first. It must be clear, then, that the work of this dispensation is solely and directly the work of the Holy Spirit. For if the Holy Spirit was the only way by which man had a holy nature and spirit at first, it is certain that fallen man, who is dead to his first holy nature, can have that same holy nature again only by the operation of the same Spirit. Indeed, the breath of the Holy Spirit was the source of man's first holy nature and life in God, and He is the source of man's regenerated holy nature and life in God.

Therefore, the direct inspiration of the Holy Spirit is as necessary to make fallen man alive again unto God as it was to create man as a living soul after the image and likeness of God. And the continual inspiration of the Spirit is as necessary as man's continuance in the redeemed state.

This is a certain truth: the power that begins or gives life must also be the only means of continuing or preserving life. No life can continue in the goodness of its first created or redeemed state except by continuing under the influence of the spirit that first created or redeemed it. Every branch of the tree, though ever so richly brought forth, must wither and die as soon as it ceases to have continual union with the root that first brought it forth.

Our Lord appealed to this truth as a proof and full illustration of the need for His indwelling, breathing, and operating in the redeemed soul of man. He said,

> *Abide in me, and I in you. As the branch cannot bear fruit of itself, except it abide in the vine; no more can ye, except ye abide in me. I am the vine, ye are the branches: he that abideth in me, and I in him, the same bringeth forth much fruit: for without me ye can do nothing. If a man abide not in me, he is cast forth as a branch, and is withered.* (John 15:4–6)

Not a Matter of Fanaticism or Pride

Now, suppose that all the words I have written here thus far are only the words of a raving fanatic.

Suppose that these words mean that turning to Christ as the Light within us, expecting life from nothing but His holy birth raised within us, giving ourselves up wholly and solely to the direct, continual filling and operation of this Holy Spirit, and depending wholly upon Him for every kind and degree of goodness and holiness, is merely pride and excessive enthusiasm. As infinitely absurd as this conclusion is, there are worse things that people can conclude. No one who condemns the continual inspiration of the Holy Spirit as extreme fanaticism is as absurd as one who concludes that, because we can do nothing without Christ, we should not expect, believe in, wait for, and depend upon His continual, direct operation in everything that we do.

Christ said, *"Without me ye can do nothing"* (John 15:5). This is the same as if He had said, "Concerning you and all that can be called your own, you are helpless in sin and misery, and nothing that is good can come from you unless it is done by the continual, direct breathing and inspiration of another Spirit. The Holy Spirit is given by God to overrule your own spirit, to save and deliver you from all your own goodness, wisdom, and learning. These things always were and always will be as corrupt and impure, as earthly and sensual, as your own fleshly nature."

Is there any selfish, creaturely pride in fully believing this to be true and in acting in full conformity to it? If so, then a beggar may as well be proud of his own wealth, although all the money that he has ever had has been given to him. Surely, there is no spiritual pride in the man who fully acknowledges that he can never have the least spark of goodness

except what is freely kindled in him by the Spirit of
God.

How can it be an expression of pride to believe
that we can never have any truth or goodness in all
that we think, say, or do unless it is brought about
solely and directly by the Spirit of God in us? If this
is pride, then, in order to have religious humility, we
must take credit for our religious virtues and deny
that we can only do good because of Christ in us. It
must also be said that Paul took too much upon himself when he said, *"'The life which I now live' is not
mine, 'but Christ liveth in me'"* (Gal. 2:20).

All Nature Bears Witness

The necessity of continual inspiration from the
Spirit of God, both to begin and to continue every
step of the divine life in man, is a truth to which
every life in nature, as well as all Scripture, bears
full witness. All natural life can subsist only when it
is directly and continually under the working power
of the root or source from which it sprang. It is the
same with the divine life in man: the divine life sub-
sists in and from God alone.

This is why resisting the Spirit, quenching the
Spirit, and grieving the Spirit give birth to every evil
that reigns in the world. These leave men and
churches not only an as easy prey, but also an inevitable prey to the Devil, the world, and the flesh.
Nothing but obedience to the Spirit, trusting in the
Spirit, walking in the Spirit, praying with and for
His continual inspiration, can possibly keep either
men or churches from being sinners or idolaters in
all that they do. For everything in the life or religion

of man that does not have the Spirit of God as its inspirer and director—no matter what it is—is earthly, sensual, and devilish.

The Power of the Gospel Is in the Spirit

When the Holy Spirit is the mover and director of something, there is great power in it. The truth and perfection of the Gospel was not shown until it became solely a ministration of the Spirit, or a kingdom in which the Holy Spirit of God could be credited for all that was done in it. While Christ was with them in the flesh, the apostles were instructed in heavenly truths from His mouth and were enabled to work miracles in His name. However, they were not yet qualified to know and teach the mysteries of His kingdom, and they did not have access to His full power.

After His resurrection, Christ conversed with them for forty days, *"speaking of the things pertaining to the kingdom of God"* (Acts 1:3). Even so, although He *"breathed on them, and saith unto them, Receive ye the Holy Ghost"* (John 20:22), they were still unable to preach or bear witness to the truth that is in Jesus. The reason for this is that a higher dispensation was still to come. This opening of the divine life in their hearts could not be brought about through merely the outward instruction of Christ Himself. He had sufficiently told His disciples the necessity of being born again of the Spirit, but He left them without this rebirth until He came again in the power of the Spirit.

He breathed on them and said, *"Receive ye the Holy Ghost"* (v. 22), yet this was not the thing itself.

This was only an outward indication of what they would receive when He, being glorified, would come again in the fullness and power of the Spirit. The Spirit would break open the deadness and darkness of their hearts with light and life from heaven. This was the only light that could and did open and verify in their souls all that Christ had said and promised to them while He was with them in the flesh.

All this was expressly declared by Christ Himself when He said unto them, *"I tell you the truth; it is expedient for you that I go away"* (John 16:7). Christ taught them to believe in and joyfully expect the coming of a higher and more blessed state than that of His bodily presence with them. He added, *"If I go not away, the Comforter will not come"* (v. 7). Therefore, the full comfort and blessing of Christ to His followers could not be had until something more was done to them and they were brought into a higher state than they could know by His verbal instructions alone.

"But if I depart," He said, *"I will send him unto you"* (John 16:7).

> When he, the Spirit of truth, is come, he will guide you into all truth....He shall glorify me [that is, He shall set up My kingdom in its glory, in the power of the Spirit]: *for he shall receive of mine, and shall show it unto you.* [I said of mine, because] *all things that the Father hath are mine.* (John 16:13–15)

When Christ told His disciples of the necessity of a higher state than the one they were in, and when He told them of the need for a comforting, illuminating Guide, He commanded them to wait in Jerusalem until they were equipped with power from on high. They could not have this Guide until Christ's outward teaching was changed into the inspiration and operation of His Spirit in their souls.

They were not yet to begin to bear witness of Him to the world from what they knew of Him in a human way—His birth, His life, His doctrines, His death, His sufferings, His resurrection, and so on. Instead, He said to them,

> *Ye shall receive power, after that the Holy Ghost is come upon you: and ye shall be witnesses unto me both in Jerusalem, and in all Judaea...and unto the uttermost part of the earth.* (Acts 1:8)

Two Fundamental Truths

Here, two fundamental truths are fully demonstrated. First, the perfection of the Gospel could not take place until Christ had been glorified and His kingdom among men had been made a continual, direct ministration of the Spirit. Everything before this was subservient and preparatory to this last dispensation, which could not have been the last if it had not carried man above types and shadows and into the real possession and enjoyment of the fullness and truth of a divine life.

For the end cannot be fulfilled until it finds the beginning. That is, the last dispensation of God to fallen man could not come until, putting an end to the bondage of *"the weak and beggarly elements"* (Gal. 4:9), it brought man to dwell in God, and God in him, as it was at the very beginning.

The second truth is that no man can have any true and real knowledge of the spiritual blessings of redemption except by the divine Spirit opening all the mysteries of a redeeming Christ. It was the same with the apostles, evangelists, and first ministers of the Gospel; and it is so from the beginning of their lifetimes to the end of the world. No man can have a divine call or a capacity to preach and bear witness of such spiritual blessings to the world unless the Holy Spirit first ministers to his heart.

The apostles were eyewitnesses to the whole life and ministry of Christ. Why, then, with their human understanding, could they not declare and testify the truth of such things until they were baptized *"with the Holy Ghost and with fire"* (Luke 3:16)? Because the truth and the mysteries of Christ's life and His redeeming act, as they may be known by man, are the very things that are accomplished by this heavenly fire and Spirit of God in our souls.

The Mystery of a Redeeming Christ

Therefore, to know the mysteries of redemption and to know the redeeming work of God in our own souls are the same thing. The one cannot be before or without the other. Every natural man, no matter who he is or how educated he is, is an entire stranger to all the mysteries of gospel redemption. He can only talk about them as he would of any other tale he has been told, until the mystery of a redeeming Christ is brought forth, verified, fulfilled, and witnessed in him by the Holy Spirit being reborn in his soul.

Redemption is entirely an inward, spiritual work. It works by altering, changing, and regenerating the life of the soul. So, it must be true that nothing but the inward state of the soul can bear true witness to the redeeming power of Christ. Redemption wholly consists in bringing forth a spiritual death of the old and a spiritual birth of the new. Thus, no one can know or believe the mysteries of Christ's redeeming power by simply knowing of or agreeing with what is said of Him in written or spoken words. Redemption comes only by inwardly finding and experiencing the operation of those mysteries by the new death and the new life, both of which must be brought about in the soul of man. Otherwise, Christ cannot be found and known by the soul as its salvation.

The Redeemed Soul

It must also be equally true that the redeemed state of the soul, which is the resurrection of a divine and holy life in it, must be the sole work of the inbreathing, creating Spirit of God, just as the first holy created state of the soul was. The mysteries of Christ's redeeming power, which bring forth the renewed state of the soul, are not earthly, finite, outward things that may be found and enjoyed by verbal descriptions or mental pictures of them. Rather, they are a spiritual operation that belongs to God alone as solely as His creating power belongs to Him.

The only thing that can redeem the soul is the same power that created the soul. The only thing that can bring forth a good thought in the soul is that which brought forth the power of thinking. And of every tendency toward goodness, no matter how small it may be, we may affirm the same thing that

Paul affirmed of his highest state: *"Yet not I, but Christ liveth in me"* (Gal. 2:20).

Again, some people claim that believing in the necessity and certainty of continual divine inspiration is wild fanaticism. In that case, the only true Christian is the one who frankly says, in order to avoid the accusation, "My own power, and not Christ's Spirit living and breathing in me, has done this for me. For if all that is good cannot be done by Christ, then whatever is good in me must have been done by my own power." Yet, how can this be?

No Middle Way

It is in vain to think that there is a middle way in this matter, and that theologians have found out what it is. Even some who deny the direct, continual inspiration of the Spirit still admit that the Spirit's "occasional influence" assists the faithful. A middle way has neither Scripture nor sense in it, for an occasional influence of the Spirit is as absurd as an occasional God, and it necessarily supposes such a God. Also, an occasional influence of the Spirit upon us calls for an occasional absence of the Spirit from us. And there could be no such thing unless God were sometimes with us and sometimes not, sometimes doing us good as the inward God of our lives, and sometimes doing us no good at all, but leaving us to be good from ourselves. The concept of occasional influence necessarily implies all this blasphemous absurdity.

Also, this middle way of an occasional influence and assistance necessarily assumes that there is something in man that is good. If it were so, the

Holy Spirit of God could not assist or cooperate with man's soul. Indeed, if there were anything good in us for God to assist and cooperate with—besides the seed of His own divine nature or His own Word of Life striving to bruise the Serpent's nature within us—it could not be true that no one is good but God. However, according to Scripture, *"there is none good but one, that is, God"* (Matt. 19:17). There is only one source of goodness, and there is only one God.

If there were any goodness in created beings besides the one goodness of the divine nature living, working, and manifesting itself in them, then creatures in both heaven and earth would have something else to adore besides God. How can anything or anyone else have a share in the adoration that is paid to the Creator? We look solely to the Spirit and depend wholly upon Him for both the beginning and the growth of every thought and desire that can be holy and good in us. The person who believes that he can have any good in him besides the goodness of God, must be worshipping another god. For God and goodness cannot be divided; therefore, all goodness in man is the result of God's Spirit within him.

Chapter 3

God within Us

There is an unchangeable distinction between God and His creation. Nature and created beings only provide an outward manifestation of the inward, invisible, unapproachable powers of God. They can rise no higher, nor can they be anything more in themselves, than temples, habitations, or instruments through which the supernatural God can manifest Himself in various degrees. He brought forth creatures to be good with His own goodness, to love and adore Him with His own Spirit of love, forever singing praises to the divine nature of which they partake.

This is the religion of divine inspiration, which is Immanuel, or God within us. Everything short of this is not the religion that worships God in spirit and in truth. When we place any religious trust or confidence in anything besides the divine operation within us, we engage in a form of idol worship, which has *"a form of godliness, but* [denies] *the power thereof"* (2 Tim. 3:5). He who places any value in theological arguments or opinions that are held about the biblical doctrines of faith, justification, sanctification, election, and reprobation, departs from the true worship of the living God within him. In fact, he sets up an idol of ideas to be worshipped, if not instead of God, then along with Him.

I believe that every group of Christians whose religion stands upon this ground, however ardent their zeal may seem to be in such matters, will sooner or later find that their evil, ungodly nature is at the bottom of it. They will soon enough discover a selfish, earthly, overbearing pride in their own definitions and doctrines. Sooner or later, this will creep up and become the same fleshly wisdom that they object to in some of the church's highest ministers. It cannot possibly be otherwise, for a zeal based solely on education can only do for Christians what it did for the Jews: it will murder the person and purposes of Christ.

The scribes, Pharisees, hypocrites, and crucifiers of Christ were all zealous in their way. Zeal such as theirs has brought forth heresies, schisms, papal decrees, and public condemnation and exclusion from church fellowship. But whether Catholic or Protestant, unholy zeal has brought about much discord and disunion, only with different materials. For instance, images of wood and clay in the Catholic church have been replaced by images of doctrines in the Protestant church. Grace and works, imputed sin and imputed righteousness, election and reprobation, have all become distorted by our human ideas of what church doctrines and practices should be.

Salvation Found Only in the Life of Jesus

This will be the condition of all fallen Christendom, whether Catholic or Protestant, until both

individuals and churches confess and firmly adhere
to the scriptural truth that our salvation is in the
life of Jesus Christ in us. This alone was the divine
perfection of man before he fell, and it will be his
perfection when he is one with Christ in heaven.

Everything besides this merely brings confusion
to the many sects and divisions of Christians who
are living according to their old natures. Anything
that does not solely aim at and lead to the life of
Christ in us, is only another theory over which so-
called holy men may contend. But this truth of
truths, fully possessed and firmly adhered to, brings
God and man together. It puts an end to every
speculation as to where the kingdom of God may be
found, and it turns the whole faith of man to a
Christ who can be a Savior to him only in the inmost
part of his being. It is not possible for Christ to be
born within man by any other means than the direct
inspiration and working power of the Holy Spirit.

Only to this spiritually reborn man does Scripture give daily edification; the words of Christ and
His apostles fall like a fire into him. What do these
words kindle there? Not ideas, not restless desires to
hear the latest teachers of them, not *"itching ears"*
(2 Tim. 4:3), but a holy flame of love to be always
with Christ and His Holy Spirit. This alone can
cause a man to be and to do all that the words of
Christ and His apostles have taught.

For there is no possibility of being like-minded
with Christ in anything that He taught, or having
the truth of even a single Christian virtue, unless
the nature and Spirit of Christ become alive in your
soul. You may read our Savior's divine Sermon on
the Mount, you may consent to the goodness of every

part of it, yet you will never practice it until you have a new nature from Christ and are as vitally in Him, and He in you, as the branch is in the vine and the vine in the branch.

"Blessed are the pure in heart: for they shall see God" (Matt. 5:8) is a divine truth, but it will do us no spiritual good unless we receive it as saying only, "Blessed are they who are born again of the Spirit, for they alone can see God." No blessed truth and no blessed life can be found either in men or in angels unless the Spirit and life of God are essentially born within them.

The Religion of Self

Individuals and churches who do not place everything in the life, light, and guidance of the Holy Spirit of Christ, but pretend to act in the name of God and for His glory, are only where the apostles were when *"there was also a strife among them, which of them should be accounted the greatest"* (Luke 22:24). Through logic and learning, many people have collected opinions from Scripture or from what various theologians have told them was right or wrong. They may boast of their great zeal for truth and the glory of God, but their own behavior toward one another is proof enough that the great strife among them is which church will be the greatest or will have the largest number of followers.

But the glory of the Christian church is not in the number of men or kingdoms professing Christianity, but in the number redeemed from the death of Adam to the life of Christ. If, by spreading the Gospel, Christianity seeks anything besides a new heavenly life through the eternal Son of God born in the fallen soul—if this spirituality of gospel redemption is denied or overlooked—then the spirit of self, of satanic and worldly trickery, will be the church and the priest and the supreme power in all that is called religion.

All along, I have been outlining the doctrine of the continual inspiration of the Spirit. In opposition to this doctrine, the natural or unregenerate man, educated in pagan learning and scholastic theology, sees the strength of his mind in his search for knowledge. He also sees how easily and learnedly he can talk, write, criticize, and make judgments upon all the words of Scripture. He looks at all this as full proof of his own religious wisdom, power, and goodness. Therefore, to his mind, the direct inspiration of the Spirit is unnecessary foolishness! Yet, he does not consider that all the things denounced by Christ against the scribes, Pharisees, and hypocrites, are the same things that his natural man practices and that are still denounced by Christ to this day.

Everyone, no matter how educated he is, is still a natural man and can have only a carnal, secular religion until the Spirit of God is fully born in him. He is as empty of everything as a newborn child until the Spirit becomes the inspirer and doer of all that he wills and does in the whole course of his life in Christ.

Our divine Master compared the religion of the learned Pharisees to *"whited sepulchres, which indeed appear beautiful outward, but are within full of dead men's bones, and of all uncleanness"* (Matt. 23:27). How could a religion, so serious in its restraints, so beautiful in its outward form and practices, and commanding such reverence from all who beheld it, be charged by Truth itself with having such an abominable nature within? Because it was only a religion of self.

Therefore, from the beginning to the end of the world, it must be true that where self is kept alive, has power, and maintains its own interests, the things that Christ condemned in the Pharisees with such severity are still alive. And the reason for such heavy condemnation is that self is the only root, or rather the sum total, of all sin. Every sin that can be named is centered in self, and every man can sin to the degree that he can live to himself. Self is the fullness of atheism and idolatry; it is nothing else but the created being that is broken off from God and Christ. Self is the power of Satan living and working in us, the sad continuation of that first turning from God that was the whole reason for the fall of our first father.

And yet, as sad and satanic as this self is, why do we cherish and nourish it with our daily love, fears, and cares about it? Man indulges in worldly wisdom and makes flattering concessions to the world so that this apostate self may have its fullness both of inward joys and outward glory.

A religion of self, of worldly glory and prosperity, that is carried on under the gospel state, has more of a diabolical nature than even the Pharisees had. It claims to deny and die to self, to be crucified with Christ, to be led by His Spirit, to be risen from the world, and to be set with Him in heavenly places, but it still lives only to self, Satan, and the world. Indeed, a religion of self is the last and greatest manifestation of the mystery of iniquity.

So then, by striving against the direct, continual inspiration of the Spirit, many people do all they can to draw others away from the very truth and perfection of the gospel state. In fact, they are no better than pitiful advocates for a religion of self, more abominable now than that which Christ condemned in the Pharisees. Whatever is pretended to be done by any other spirit or power besides the Holy Spirit—whether praying, preaching, or practicing religious duties—is only the religion of self, and can be nothing else.

All that is *"born of the flesh is flesh"* (John 3:6), and nothing is spiritual but that which is entirely from the Spirit. When man is not ruled and governed by the Spirit, he has only the nature of corrupt flesh, is under the full power and guidance of his fallen nature, and is that very natural man to whom the things of God are foolishness (1 Cor. 2:14). But the man who boldly rejects and preaches against a direct, continual inspiration of the Spirit is an anti-apostle. Indeed, he lays another foundation than that which Christ has laid. Such a man teaches that Christ does not need or want to be all in all in us, and he preaches that being afraid to grieve, quench, and resist the Holy Spirit is pure foolishness. But this man is the fool!

The Unpardonable Sin

Not one of us would ever be in danger of grieving, quenching, or resisting the Spirit if His holy breathings and inspirations were always within us. Sinning against the Holy Spirit would not be more dreadful than sinning against the Father and the Son, if it were not for the fact that the direct, continual guidance and operation of the Spirit is the last and highest manifestation of the Holy Trinity in the fallen soul of man. It is not that the Holy Spirit is worthier or higher in nature than the Father and the Son, but that Father and Son come forth to redeem us through a covenant of the continual inspiration of the Spirit, to be always dwelling and working in our souls.

Many things have been conjectured and published to the world about the sin against the Holy Spirit, but the whole nature of it lies in the fact that it is a sin against the last and highest dispensation of God for the full redemption of man. Christ said, *"If I had not come...they had not had sin"* (John 15:22). In other words, man would not have such a weight of guilt upon him. Sinning against Christ in the flesh is more unpardonable than sinning against the Father under the law. However, sinning against the Holy Spirit is more unpardonable than sinning against the Father under the law or sinning against the Son who came in the flesh. This is because the two preceding dispensations were only preparations for the full ministration of the Spirit.

But now that both the Father and the Son have come in the power and manifestation of the Spirit, then he who refuses or resists this ministration of the Spirit also resists all that the Trinity can do to restore and revive the first life of God in his soul. And so, he who resists and rejects the Spirit of God also commits the unpardonable sin, which is unpardonable because there remains no further or higher power to remove it from the soul.

Keep in mind that sin is only pardonable if there is something higher that can remove it from the soul. And no sin can be unpardonable unless it has withstood or turned from the last and highest remedy for the removal of it.

Thus, grieving, quenching, or resisting the Spirit is the sin of all sins, the sin that most of all stops the work of redemption and separates man from all union with God. But there could be no such sin unless the Holy Spirit could be always breathing, willing, and working within us. What spirit can be grieved by us but One whose will is disobeyed within us? What spirit can be quenched by us but One that is and always will be a holy fire of life within us? What spirit can be resisted by us but One that operates within us? A spirit on the outside of us cannot be the Spirit of God, nor could such a spirit be quenched or hindered by our spirits any more than a man could stop a storm by his indignation.

The Knowledge of God Is Life

Now, as dreadful as the aforementioned sin is, I wonder whether those who are against the continual divine inspiration of the Spirit are, by such a doctrine, actually leading people into a habitual state of sinning against the Holy Spirit. For if we do not continually reverence His holy presence within us, how can we possibly avoid the sins of grieving, quenching, or resisting the Spirit? Unless we continually wait for, trust in, and solely give heed to all that the Spirit of God wills, works, and manifests within us, how can we avoid sinning against the Holy Spirit?

When someone turns people away from this continual dependence upon the Holy Spirit, he also turns them away from all true knowledge of God.

Without the Spirit, there is no possibility of any edi-
fying, saving knowledge of God. We may have many
empirical demonstrations of His existence, but we
have no real knowledge of Him until His own Spirit
within us manifests Him as a power of life, light,
love, and goodness. He is to be truly found, vitally
felt, and adored in our souls.

This knowledge of God is eternal life because it
is the life of God manifested in the soul. It is the
knowledge of which Christ said, *"No man knoweth...
the Father, save the Son, and he to whomsoever the
Son will reveal him"* (Matt. 11:27). This knowledge
is found only in those who are new creatures in
Christ, for the rebirth is the way in which Christ re-
veals the Father. But if none belong to God except
those who are led by the Spirit of God—if we are
reprobates unless the Spirit of Christ lives in us—do
we need to be told that, as children of God and
Christ, we must depend solely upon the direct, continual guidance and teaching of this Holy Spirit
within us?

How can we more profanely sin against this
Spirit and power of God within us, how can we more
directly call men away from the power of God to the
power of Satan, than by ridiculing the faith and hope
that look completely to Him for all that can be holy
and good in us?

"I, if I be lifted up from the earth," said Christ,
"will draw all men unto me" (John 12:32). The one
great power of Christ in and over the souls of men
came after He ascended into heaven. His ascension
brought the true, full power of His drawing, because
it is by His Spirit in man that He draws men to
Himself. But who can do more to resist this drawing

or to defeat its operation in us than he who preaches
against the continual and direct inspiration of the
Spirit? Let us remember that Christ's drawing cannot occur or be powerful in any other way than by
the Holy Spirit in man.

Chapter 4

Entire Dependence
upon the Spirit

The whole purpose of the Scriptures is to draw us to God through Jesus Christ. Everything that the Bible says, no matter how it is read or studied by scholars, fails in its purpose until it brings us to God within us. All that the Scriptures say about God, man, life and death, good and evil, heaven and hell, needs to be verified in our own souls. God within us means divine life, divine light, and divine love, but Satan within us is the life of self, earthly wisdom, diabolical falseness, wrath, pride, and vanity of every kind.

There is no middle way between these two. Anyone who is not under the power of the one is under the power of the other. The reason for this is that man was created in and under the power of the divine life; therefore, the more he loses or turns away from this life of God, the more he falls under the power of self, Satan, and worldly wisdom. When Peter, full of human love toward Christ, advised Him to avoid His sufferings, Christ rejected him with, *"Get thee behind me, Satan"* (Matt. 16:23). Christ gave only this reason for it: *"For thou savourest not*

the things that be of God, but those that be of men"
(v. 23).

We find further evidence of this by observing
that whatever is not of and from the Holy Spirit of
God in us, however plausible it may seem to man's
outward wisdom and natural goodness, is in itself
the power of Satan within us.

Paul said of himself, *"By the grace of God I am
what I am"* (1 Cor. 15:10). Likewise, every so-called
wise man, everyone who trusts the strength of his
own rational learning, everyone who is under the
power of his own fallen nature—never free from desires for honor and recognition, ever thirsting to be
rewarded for his theological abilities, ever fearing to
be abased and despised, always thankful to those
who flatter him with his distinguished merit—
everyone who is like this may truly say of himself,
"Because I turned to and trusted in something other
than the grace and inspiration of God's Spirit, I am
what I am." This is the only thing that hinders a believer from being able to say with Paul, *"God forbid
that I should glory, save in the cross of our Lord Jesus Christ, by whom the world is crucified unto me,
and I unto the world"* (Gal. 6:14).

A religion of self makes one incapable of finding
what Paul found when he said, *"I can do all things
through Christ which strengtheneth me"* (Phil. 4:13).
Choosing to have a religion of self, worldly learning,
and human greatness, rather than to be a "fool for
Christ," hinders the life of Christ in our souls. The
man who disregards the necessity of having Christ
within will not renounce everything that Jesus renounced, but will seek the earthly honor and praise
that Christ never sought. Such a man does not

humble himself to will nothing, know nothing, and seek nothing but what the Spirit of God and Christ wills, knows, and seeks in him.

The Spirit Brings Life to Religion

Here, and here alone, lies the Christian's full and certain power of overcoming self, the Devil, and the world. But if Christians turn to anything else besides the one Spirit of God and Christ in order to be led and inspired, they will bring forth a Christianity that in God's sight will be a spiritual Babylon, a spiritual Egypt and Sodom, a scarlet whore, a devouring beast, and a red dragon. All these names belong to all men, however educated they are, and to all churches, whether large or small, in which the spirit of this world has any power.

This is where the church went wrong soon after the apostolic ages. All human reformations, begun by ecclesiastical learning and supported by civil power, will mean little or nothing in the end. Indeed, they often make things worse, until all churches, dying to all their own will, wisdom, and advancement, seek only the reforming power of the Spirit of God, who converted sinners, publicans, harlots, Jews, and heathens into the first apostolical church. The early church knew that they were of God, that they belonged to God, because the Spirit had been given to them and had begun to work in them.

"Ye are not in the flesh," said the apostle, *"but in the Spirit"* (Rom. 8:9). But then he added, as the only basis for this, *"If so be that the Spirit of God dwell in you"* (v. 9). Surely he meant, "If you are moved, guided, and governed by that which the

Spirit wills, works, and inspires within you." And then, to show the absolute necessity of this life of God in the soul, he added, *"If any man have not the Spirit of Christ, he is none of his"* (v. 9).

We know that this is the state to which God has called all Christians, because Paul said, *"God hath sent forth the Spirit of his Son into your hearts, crying, Abba, Father"* (Gal. 4:6). It is as if he had said, "Nothing in you can cry or pray to God as its Father unless the Spirit of His Son Jesus comes to life in you." This is also true of every tendency in the soul toward God or goodness. The more of such tendencies we have, the more Christ, the "seed of the woman," strives to bring forth a full new birth in our souls.

"Lo, I am with you alway," said our holy Lord, *"even unto the end of the world"* (Matt. 28:20). How is He with us? Even an uneducated man knows that He is not with us in the flesh. Many theologians say that He is not within our physical bodies, because having the literal body of Christ within us would be as absurd as our carrying a shining light inside our own stomachs. How, then, can the common Christian find any comfort in these words of Christ's promise, unless the Spirit brings him into a remembrance and belief that Christ is in him and with him, as the vine is in and with the branch?

Christ Working in and with Us

Christ said, *"Without me ye can do nothing"* (John 15:5). He also said, *"If a man love me...my Father will love him, and we will come unto him, and make our abode with him"* (John 14:23). Now, if we can do nothing without Him, then all the love that we can possibly have for Christ must be from the power and life of Christ in us. As a result of this love, we have the Father and the Son dwelling and making their abode in us. Do we need any greater proof that the whole work of redemption in the soul of man is the direct, inward, continual operation of Father, Son, and Holy Spirit, raising up again the life of holiness to which our first father died?

Following His glorification in heaven, Christ said, *"Behold, I stand at the door, and knock"* (Rev. 3:20). He did not say, "Behold, you have me in the Scriptures; that is enough." What is the door at which Christ, at the right hand of God in heaven, still knocks? Surely it is the heart, to which Christ is always present. He went on, *"If any man hear my voice"* (v. 20). How can a man hear His voice except by listening with his heart? What voice is heard but the voice of Christ within him? Christ added, *"And open the door* [meaning, "will open his heart for Me"], *I will come in to him"* (v. 20). That is, if a man will have a living, holy nature and will have the Spirit born within him, Christ *"will sup with him, and he with* [Christ]*"* (v. 20).

This is the last, finishing work of a redeeming Jesus, who enters into the heart that opens to Him. He brings forth the joy, the blessing, and the perfection of that first life of God in the soul. This perfection was lost by the Fall, and it was set forth as a supper, or a feast of the heavenly Jesus with the soul, and the soul with Him. Can anyone justly call it fanaticism if a man's soul communes with this glorified Christ within him? Can anyone say that this does not mean that something has transacted in the soul that is more heavenly than the Last Supper, which Jesus celebrated with His disciples while He was with them in flesh?

The Last Supper was an outward symbol of the inward and blessed nourishment on which the believing soul will feast when the glorified Son of God enters into it and raises up His heavenly nature and life within it. As Christ continually knocks at the door of the heart, He sets forth the nature of a direct, continual, divine inspiration within us. It is always with us, but our hearts must open up to it. And though it is always there, it is only felt and found by those who are attentive to it, who depend upon and humbly wait for it.

Now, how can anyone believe anything of this voice of Christ, how can he listen to it, hear it, or obey it, without a faith that keeps him always attuned to the direct and constant inspiration of the Spirit of Christ within him? How can any profane person do more damage to this presence and power of Christ in his own soul, than by making a mockery of the light within, the Christ within? Who can lead more people away from God than the so-called Christian who openly blasphemes the faith, hope, and trust that rely solely upon the move of the Spirit to do what is right and pious toward both God and man?

If this is what you have been doing, take to heart what I say. Time and the things of time will soon come to an end, and anyone who does not trust the Spirit and power of God working in his heart will not be prepared to enter into eternity. God must be our all in all here, or else we cannot belong to Him hereafter. Time works only toward eternity, and eternal poverty will as certainly befall the man who dies full of only human learning as he who dies full of only worldly riches.

It is foolish to think that we can have any divine learning besides that which the Holy Spirit teaches. We cannot make ourselves rich in knowledge toward God. The foolishness of it will leave us as dreadfully cheated as the rich builder of barns in the Gospel, to whom it was said, *"Thou fool, this night thy soul shall be required of thee: then whose shall those things be?"* (Luke 12:20). Every man who treasures the religious learning that does not come wholly from the Spirit of God, is the same as this foolish man.

Both God and Satan at Work

The writer of Hebrews called us to give ongoing attention to the continual working of the Holy Spirit within us:

> *See that ye refuse not him that speaketh. For if they escaped not who refused him that spake on earth, much more shall not we escape, if we turn away from him that speaketh from heaven.*
> *(Heb. 12:25)*

Now, what is this speaking from heaven, which is so dangerous to refuse or resist? Surely it is not audible voices from heaven! This passage could only mean a voice from heaven that we are always either inwardly obeying or inwardly refusing.

James said, *"Resist the devil, and he will flee from you"* (James 4:7). What Devil? Surely he is not a creature in the physical sense, or a spirit who tempts us by an outward power. How can we resist the Devil except by inwardly turning from the workings of his evil nature and spirit within us? Those who tell us to stop waiting for, depending upon, and giving heed to the continual, secret inspiration and breathing of the Holy Spirit within us, are telling us to resist God in the same manner as we have been exhorted to resist the Devil. How absurd!

God is spiritual good, and the Devil is spiritual evil. We could not resist either of them if we could not also obey their spiritual operations within us. James showed us that resisting the Devil is the only way to make him flee from us, that is, to get rid of his power in us. He then showed us how we are to behave toward God, so that He may not flee from us and so that His holy work will not be stopped in us. *"Draw nigh to God,"* he said, *"and he will draw nigh to you"* (James 4:8).

What does it mean to draw near to God? Surely it does not imply any physical motion, either in God or in us. But it is just as if James had said, "Do not resist God. Let His holy will within you have its full work. Remain wholly and obediently attentive to all that He is and has and does within you, and then God will draw near to you. That is, He will more and more manifest the power of His holy presence in you and will make you more and more a partaker of the divine nature."

The Teaching of the Church

Those who accuse people of fanaticism for believing in the necessity and certainty of such direct, continual inspiration, must be blind to the Spirit. Indeed, these accusers say that certain believers are enemies of the church, when everybody can plainly see that prayer after prayer in the established liturgy requires them to believe in and pray for the continual inspiration of the Spirit. The church teaches that the Spirit is the only way by which believers can have even the smallest good thought or desire.

One prayer says, "O God, forasmuch as without Thee we are not able to please Thee, mercifully grant that Thy Holy Spirit may in all things direct and rule our hearts." Is it possible for words to express more strongly the necessity of continual divine inspiration from the Spirit of God? Was the inspiration in the prophets and apostles any higher than that which directs and rules our hearts in all things today? Or can the absolute necessity of this inspiration be more fully declared than by saying that we cannot please God or have any union with Him without the divine inspiration of the Spirit?

I must interject here that the matter is not at all about the different effects or works proceeding from divine inspiration. It is not really about whether a man is made a saint or is sent out as a missionary by divine inspiration. This does not affect the nature and necessity of having the Holy Spirit in our souls. Divine inspiration is as necessary to salvation and godliness as it is to preaching the Word.

All Scripture is inspired by God (2 Tim. 3:16). Why? Because *"holy men of God spake as they were moved by the Holy Ghost"* (2 Pet. 1:21). In a similar manner, the teachings of Christ and His apostles oblige us to believe that all holiness is by divine inspiration, and that therefore there could have been no holy men in any age unless they also lived *"as they were moved by the Holy Ghost."*

There is a prayer that says, "O God, from whom all good things do come, grant that by Thy holy inspiration we may think the things that are good, and by Thy merciful guiding may perform the same." Now, if I have ever said anything contradictory to what this prayer says about the nature and necessity of continual divine inspiration, I will refuse no judgment that may be passed upon me.

But if, from all that we know about God, nature, and man, I have shown that no degree of goodness can be in us unless we have the divine nature living and breathing in us; if I have shown that Scripture, Christ, and His apostles say the same thing over and over, then those who accuse me of being a fanatic will hear from me exactly what Christ said of His blind crucifiers: *"Father, forgive them; for they know not what they do"* (Luke 23:34).

The Abuse of This Doctrine

It is fruitless to object to this teaching by pointing to Christians who act wildly under the pretense of being called and led by the Spirit. Whether their actions and beliefs are true or not, it is a matter that does not require our meddling. The doctrines that we stand upon are not affected by their behavior in the least.

Even if radicals of the present and former ages have abused the doctrine of being led by the Spirit of God, people still could not say, "He who preaches the doctrine of being led by the Spirit of God is a fanatic, or he helps to promote the radical cause." This would be an illogical argument. But, as absurd as this is, if the accusers would consider the logic of what I say, they would not be able to present a stronger argument than this to prove that I am a fanatic or a promoter of such radical things.

I am told that, under a pretense of having a regard for religion and supposedly for the sake of it, whole nations and churches have done all the things that anyone can be accused of regarding fanaticism. You may know these things as schisms, perjury, rebellion, deception, hypocrisy, and so on. But I do not begin to doubt the necessity, the truth, and the perfection of gospel doctrines simply on the basis of these evils.

I know that both spiritual pride and fleshly lusts have prospered under the pretense of people being led by the Spirit. Satan has often led people into all the heights of self-glory and self-seeking under the deception that they were being inspired with gospel humility and self-denial. Nevertheless, I do not give up the necessity, the truth, and the perfection of looking wholly to the Spirit of God and Christ within me as my promised inspirer and the only worker of all that can be good in me.

Chapter 5

Reason and Religion

A nother charge that has been brought against me, which is equally false and far more senseless, is that I am an enemy of the use of reason in religion. Why? Because in all my writings I teach that reason is to be denied. I admit that I have not only taught this, but I have again and again proved the absolute necessity of it. I do this because Christ has made it absolutely necessary by saying, *"If any man will come after me, let him deny himself"* (Matt. 16:24).

How can a man deny himself without denying his reason, unless reason is not a part of him? Or how can a rational creature, whose chief distinction from the beasts is his reason, be called to deny himself in any other way than by denying that which is distinctive about him? Let us suppose, then, that man is not to deny his reason. What happens then? He is told to deny himself but not his reason.

Natural Reason Must Be Denied

Have you ever heard such nonsense? My accusers say that the doctrine of denying self is wise and good, but then they insist that denying one's reason is bad. But how can a man deny himself except by denying that which is the life and spirit and power of self? What makes a man a sinner? Nothing but the power and working of his natural reason. Therefore, if our natural reason is not to be denied, we will maintain the very thing that brings about every sin that ever was or can be in us.

Now, when I speak of natural reason, I mean only the natural man. This is the same thing Paul intended when he wrote,

> But the natural man receiveth not the things of the Spirit of God: for they are foolishness unto him: neither can he know them, because they are spiritually discerned. *(1 Cor. 2:14)*

We would not sin at all if our natural reason or understanding had no power in us. What do the Scriptures mean by the phrase, *"the works of the flesh"* (Gal. 5:19)? Are they something distinct and different from the workings of our rational and intelligent nature? No, the flesh and the carnal man are comprised of our intelligent, rational nature. In fact, the carnal man's intelligence or reason makes his carnality all the more evil, even more so than the beasts. Everything that our Lord said about the self was also said concerning our natural reason, and all that the Scriptures say about the flesh and its evil nature is also said concerning the evil state of our natural reason. Therefore, our natural reason must be denied in the same manner and degree that self and the flesh must be denied.

Many Bible scholars are ignorant of the most fundamental truths of the Gospel in regard to the fall of man and the new birth. In addition, they are ignorant concerning the doctrine of denying oneself, which modern learning supposes to be possible without, or different from, denying one's own natural reason. This is an absurdity of the greatest magnitude.

Is self not what a man is and has in his natural capacity? Is the extent of his natural understanding not the strength and power of his reason? How, then, can any man deny himself without denying that which gives self its nature, name, and power? If man were not a rational creature, he could not be called to deny himself, nor could he receive any benefit or goodness from self-denial. Therefore, no man can obey the precept of denying himself, or have any benefit or goodness from it, but insofar as he denies, or dies to, his own natural reason. The self of man, and the natural reason of man, are exactly the same thing.

Our blessed Lord said in His agony, *"Not my will, but thine, be done"* (Luke 22:42). This was the pattern of His whole life, and He lived without sin. Likewise, to the degree that we stay away from our own natural wills, we will stay away from sin. The height of our calling is to deny our own wills, so that God's will alone may be done in us.

But now, if our own natural wills, with all the sin and evil in them, are always to be denied, no matter what it costs us, how can our natural reason not be included in this as well? How can we deny our own wills and not deny the rational or intelligent powers from which our wills derive their whole existence and continual direction? How can there always be an evil in our own wills without such an evil affecting our natural intellectual powers?

Therefore, it is absolutely certain that the more we deny our own natural wills, the more the will of God will be done in us. We must deny our own natural reason and understanding if we do not wish to follow our own wills. For whoever lives according to his own natural reason also lives according to his own natural will. Our natural wills are nothing more than our natural reasoning powers willing one thing or another in us.

The Way to Divine Knowledge

Now, to those with an unregenerate nature, this may seem difficult to understand. It is even harder for educated men to understand. Yet, as certainly as man fell in the Garden of Eden, this full denial of our own natural wills and our own natural reason is the only possible way for divine knowledge, divine light, and divine goodness to have any place or power in us. All other religious knowledge, obtained in any other way, no matter how great it is, is only great in vanity, emptiness, and delusion. Only what comes directly from God can have any godliness in it.

Anything that comes from self and natural reason, however it may appear externally, is actually of no better a nature than self-seeking, self-satisfaction, and fleshly wisdom. These are the very works of the Devil in us, which Christ came into the world to destroy. Any efforts of natural reason to be great in religious knowledge are as satanic as anything else that places us in a state that is contrary to what our Lord affirmed to be absolutely necessary.

Christ said, *"Except ye be converted, and become as little children, ye shall not enter into the kingdom of heaven"* (Matt. 18:3). No one can be converted in this manner, or come under the good influence of this childlike nature, until natural reason, self, and the will are all equally denied. For all the evil and corruption of our fallen nature comes into view when our own reason is awakened, when our own wills are broken off from God, and when we have fallen into the selfish workings of our own earthly nature.

Now, whether this self that is broken off from God attempts to reason, will, and contend over scriptural words and opinions, or whether it reasons against them all, the same evil state of fallen nature, the same loss of life, the same separation from God, the same evil nature of flesh and blood, will be equally strengthened and inflamed. Catholics and Protestants have hated, fought, and killed one another for the sake of their different opinions, yet they have been in the highest union and communion with one another as to the lust of the flesh, the lust of the eye, and the pride of life (1 John 2:16).

This is why Christendom, full of the nicest sayings about faith, grace, works, merits, satisfactions, heresies, schisms, and so on, is also full of all the evil tendencies that prevailed in the heathen world when none of the things of God were ever thought of.

Picture a scholar who pities the blindness and folly of those who live to themselves in the cares and pleasures of this vain life. He thinks that he is divinely employed, that he has escaped the pollution of the world, because day after day he is dividing, dissecting, and mending church opinions, fixing heresies here, schisms there. Meanwhile, he forgets that the carnal self and man's natural reason are responsible for all that is accomplished by his learned zeal. He forgets that such things are as busy and active in him as they are in the reasoning infidel or worldling.

But now imagine a scholar who has wholly denied self. He can only be accused of heresy, schism, and wickedness if he does not love God with his whole heart, and his neighbors as himself. All that can be called truth, life, or salvation in such a man is the Spirit, nature, and power of Christ living and manifesting themselves in him, as they did in Christ. However, no matter how great a scholar he is, the more he allows self or the natural man to become great in religious learning, the more he will be fixed in false religion.

How Reason Should Be Used

Having written all this, I certainly do not deny the use of reason in religion, and I wish to refute any accusation to that effect. In fact, I have for a long time maintained the same doctrine on this subject.

I will grant that reason has as great a share in the good things of religion as it has in the things of this natural life. Reason can assist the soul as much as it can assist the body. It has the same power and virtue in the spiritual that it has in the natural world. It can communicate to us as much of the one as of the other, and it is of the same usefulness and importance in the one as in the other. Can you ask for more than this?

Man is a part of this world and is to have his share of the good that is in it. Man is a sensible and a rational creature. He has a certain number of senses—seeing, hearing, tasting, touching, and smelling—by which he is aware of what the outward world, in which he is placed, can do for him or communicate to him. Therefore, he is aware of what kind and degree of happiness he can derive from it. But in addition to these sensory organs, man can reason upon the ideas that he receives from these senses.

How are the good things of this world communicated to man? How can he possess them? To what part of him are they proposed? Are his senses, or is his reason, the means by which he can have the things of this world?

If we lower reason in regard to religion, then we are obliged to set it just as low with respect to the things of this world. Reason is no more the means of communicating the good things of the natural world than of the spiritual world. Paul said, *"The natural man receiveth not the things of the Spirit of God...because they are spiritually discerned"* (1 Cor. 2:14). Similarly, the rational man cannot receive the things of this world because they are received by the sense organs.

Reason has no higher office or power in the things of this world than it has in the things of religion. It does not see, hear, taste, or feel the things of this life; it can take the place of none of these senses. It is just as helpless and useless in religion; it cannot see, hear, taste, or feel spiritual things. Therefore, in the things of religion and in the things of this world, it has the same insignificance. The soul must receive what this world can communicate to it; the spirit must receive what God can communicate. Reason may follow in either case, and see in its own mirror what is done, but it can do no more.

Reason has the same role in religion that it has when we desire any of the enjoyments of this life. Reason may show us how and where we can find them; it may tell us to remove a covering from our eyes or open our window shutters when we want the light; but it can do no more toward seeing than to make way for the light to fall upon our eyes. This is also its capacity in the things of religion. It may remove the thing that hinders the awareness of the soul, or it may prevent the divine light from acting upon it, but it can do no more.

The Good of Reason

The faculty of reason is only the activity of the mind upon its own ideas or images, which the senses have caused it to form from what has been stirred up in them. Reason does not become dark when it ponders the cause or nature of darkness, nor does it become light when it thinks about the sun. Thus, reason is not religion, nor does it have any of the qualities of religion, even when it reflects on various descriptions and definitions of religious doctrines and virtues.

The good of religion is like the good of food and drink to the person who is hungry or thirsty. However, if, instead of giving him bread and wine, you taught him to seek relief by clearly understanding the nature of bread, or by knowing different ways of making it, he would be left to die of starvation. In the same way, a religion that consists entirely of reason leaves the soul to perish because it lacks the good that can be found in true religion.

Of course, sometimes the benefit of food is greatly assisted by the right use of one's reason.

Reason does not have the good of food in it, but
many people have food to eat because they know
how to go about getting or preparing it. Likewise, a
man may secure for himself the good of religion by
the right use of his reason, even though reason does
not have the good of religion in it. It would be great
foolishness to accuse a man of being an enemy of the
true use of reasoning about food because he declares that reason is not food. It is equally foolish to
accuse a man of being an enemy of the use of reason in religion because he declares that reason is
not religion.

Our only lack in living out our faith is our need
to have more of the divine nature in us than we have
of our fallen nature. If this is the truth of the matter
(and who can deny it?), then we can be sure that the
only good in religion comes from that which communicates to us something of God, or which alters our
state of existence in God and makes us partakers of
the divine nature in the way that is needed.

We Should Trust Only in God

Is it not therefore foolish to put any trust in a
religion of rational ideas and opinions that have
been logically deduced from words of Scripture?
Sinners of all sorts, and men under the power of
every corrupt passion, are zealous for such a religion. This ought to be proof enough that reason does
not have the good of religion in it; it does not kill
any of the vices of the heart, nor is it killed by
them. Pride, hypocrisy, envy, and malice do not
take away the mind's critical abilities. Thus, a man
may be most logical in his religion of reason, words,

doctrines, and opinions, even when he has none of the true good of religion in him, but all of his natural vices.

However, once people discover that all happiness or misery is proportional to how much a person is possessed by God, then it must be equally known that no power besides God can be any religious good to them. As it becomes known that happiness depends upon how much one partakes of the divine nature, it will also be known that God cannot be any religious good to us except by the communication of Himself or the manifestation of His own life within us. By this we see that both infidels and Christians can be equally blind. The one group trusts its own reason concerning logical conclusions; the other trusts its own reason regarding educated opinions about scriptural words and phrases, and doctrines built upon them.

We must know and confess that God is all in all. We must know that *"in him we live, and move, and have our being"* (Acts 17:28), that we can have nothing while we are apart from Him, but everything in Him. We must know that we have no life or degree of life except in Him; that He can give us nothing as our good besides Himself; that salvation can come into our fallen nature only to the degree that He again communicates something more of Himself to us. As soon as these things are known, then it will be known with the utmost assurance that putting religious trust in our own reason, whether confined to itself or working in doctrines about words of Scripture, is the same as the idolatry that puts a religious trust in the sun, a departed saint, or a graven image.

Image-worship has often boasted of its divine power, due to the zeal and devotion that have been raised by it in thousands and tens of thousands of its followers. Therefore, it is no marvel that opinion-worship often boasts of the same effects. But the truth of the whole matter lies here: the Word, who was manifested in the flesh, that is, who became man, is the one Mediator, the Restorer of union between God and man. It must be evident, then, that nothing but this one mediatory nature of Christ, brought to life in our souls, can be our salvation. Truly, the salvation of every man and woman in the world can be found in that which saved and exalted the humanity in which Christ dwelt.

Chapter 6

The Light of
the Spirit

So many people are deluded by worldly knowledge concerning divine inspiration. But, if they would only remember a single saying either of Christ or His apostles concerning the Holy Spirit and His operations, they would see that their pursuit of knowledge is in vain. For every word that Christ or His apostles ever said fully shows that all knowledge or perception of the Spirit is also the enjoyment of the Spirit, and no man can know more of the Spirit than what the Spirit Himself manifests of His power in man.

"The things of God," said Paul, *"knoweth no man, but the Spirit of God"* (1 Cor. 2:11). Is this not conclusive? Is this not proof enough that only the Spirit of God in man can know what the Spirit's work does in man? The fruits of the Spirit, so often mentioned in Christian circles, are not different or separate from the Spirit; and if the Spirit is not always working in us, His fruits must be as absent from us as He is. John wrote, *"Hereby we know that he abideth in us, by the Spirit which he hath given*

us" (1 John 3:24), and so we understand that the Spirit can make Himself known to us only by dwelling and working in us.

James said, *"Every good gift and every perfect gift is from above"* (James 1:17). When an individual seeks the highest gift of knowledge from below, from the poor contrivance of a commonplace book, does he not therefore deny this Scripture? *"If any of you lack wisdom, let him ask of God"* (v. 5). James did not say, "Let him ask Peter or Paul or John," because he knew that divine wisdom is divine inspiration and nothing else. It can only come from above.

Some people consult the writings of all sorts of eminent and judicious authors, writers who seem to know much about virtue and morality. But all the knowledge that we can have of God must come solely from the Spirit and the enjoyment of the Spirit, for only the Holy Spirit can know the things of God. This is a truth, taught not only by all Scripture, but also by the whole nature of things.

Everything that can be seen, known, heard, felt, and so on, must be manifested by itself, and not by anything else. It is not possible for anything but light to manifest light, or for anything but darkness to cause darkness to be known. Yet it would be more possible for these things to happen than for anything but divine inspiration to cause divine inspiration to be known. If a person were to consult some ingenious and eminent atheist about the truth and certainty of God's direct, continual providence, he would be quite a fool. Or, if he were to ask a few selected Deists how or what he ought to believe concerning the nature and power of gospel faith, he would prove that he is not in his right mind.

The Only Real Interpreter of Scripture

The truth is, there are the Holy Spirit's own operations, and there are reports about them. The only true reports are those made by individuals inspired by God. If there were no such people, there could be no true reports of the Spirit's operations. Therefore, to consult uninspired people concerning the truth about direct and continual divine inspiration, or to confer with those who deny and reproach the claim of the inspiration of the Spirit, is a degree of blindness greater than could have been charged upon the old Jewish scribes and Pharisees.

The reports that are to be acknowledged as true concerning the Holy Spirit and His operations, are those that are recorded in Scripture. In other words, the Scriptures are an infallible history or account of what the Holy Spirit is, does, and works in true believers. The Scriptures are also an infallible manual on how we are to seek, wait, and trust in His good power over us. But the Scriptures themselves, though they are true and infallible in these reports and instructions about the Holy Spirit, can be no more than a true history. They cannot give to the reader of them the deeper meaning, the awareness, and the enjoyment of what they relate.

This is clear not only from the nature of a written history, but also from the words spoken by our Lord. He said, *"Except a man be born of water and of the Spirit, he cannot enter into the kingdom of God"* (John 3:5). The new birth from above, or of the Spirit, is the only thing that gives the true knowledge and perception of the kingdom of God. A written history may relate many truths about it, but the kingdom of God, dwelling and ruling in our souls as the power and presence of God, can only manifest itself to man through the new birth. Everything else in man is deaf, dumb, and blind to the kingdom of God. However, when that which died in Adam (this being the birth that came at first from God) is made alive again by the quickening Spirit from above, a man may partake of the divine nature, and he may know and enjoy the kingdom of God.

"I am the way, the truth, and the life" (John 14:6), said Christ. This record of Scripture is true, but what a delusion for a man to think that he knows the truth of this, and knows that Christ is all this benefit and blessing to him, simply because he consents to and perhaps even contends for the truth of those words! This is impossible! The new birth is the only power of entrance to God's kingdom; everything else knocks at the door in vain. *"I know you not"* (Matt. 25:12), says Christ to everything but the new birth. *"I am the way, the truth and the life"* tells us neither more nor less than if Christ had said, "I am the kingdom of God, into which nothing can enter but that which is born of the Spirit."

By this, the absolute necessity of direct and divine inspiration throughout every part of the Christian life may be seen. For if a birth of the Spirit is the only thing that can enable us to enter into or receive the kingdom of God and the only thing that can reveal Christ to be the way, the truth, and the life, then a continual life or breathing of the Spirit in us is as necessary as the first birth of the Spirit was to our creation.

Birth is only the beginning of life, and so a birth of the Spirit is only the beginning of life in the

Spirit. Therefore, if the life of the Spirit does not continue, then the birth is lost, and the cessation of its breathing in us is nothing but death again to the kingdom of God, to everything that is or can be godly. The direct, continual inspiration of the Spirit, as the only possible power and preservation of a godly life, is as absolutely necessary to salvation as the new birth—because they are one and the same!

Knowledge versus the Breath of the Spirit

If this power and life of the Spirit is not the one life of all that is done in a church, then that church is nothing in the sight of God but a group of wise Greeks and carnal Jews turned into a body of water-baptized Christians. If the working of the Spirit were taken away from the church, the church would have no power, no matter how outwardly glorious or full of educated members it may be. For until a man is born of and led by the Spirit of God, everything about him belongs to the kingdom of this world, in which Satan is declared to be the prince.

How poor and miserable is the man who strives, with all the strategies of human intelligence, to be delivered from the direct, continual operation and governance of the Spirit of God! Does he not know that the Devil is always where God is not, and that the work of the flesh is in every place where the Spirit does not rule? Even where nothing but spiritual and Christian matters are talked about, the Devil can still come in if God is not the God of everything and everyone. Indeed, the natural man can talk and express ideas and opinions about Scripture;

in these he may be a great critic, an acute logician, a powerful public speaker, and know everything about the facts of Scripture. However, if he is missing the Spirit of God, he is missing the truth.

It is to be lamented, and we cannot deny, that among nearly all educated Christians, the true and proper means of attaining divine knowledge is thought to be something that every natural, selfish, proud, envious, false, vain, worldly man can utilize. Though all of Scripture assures us that the things of the Spirit of God are foolishness to the natural man, and will be until the end of the world, people continually look to natural means of gaining knowledge about God.

Too often, students of divinity are taught to partake of the light of the Gospel just as they would of pagan writers, whether poets, novelists, or comedians. That is, they are taught to exercise the same logic and critical skill in studying the Scriptures as they would exercise in studying Shakespeare. In this way, the students, and others, think that they have gained sufficient apostolic knowledge. Is it any wonder, therefore, if the very same vain, corrupt, puffed-up literature that raises one man to be a poet laureate, sometimes sets another in a high position in the church?

How does the logical, critical, educated Deist become an infidel? By using the same good powers of the natural man through which many educated Christians come to know, embrace, and contend for the faith of the Gospel. If we dismiss the power and reality of divine inspiration, then everything that can set the believer above the infidel is also dismissed.

The Spirit Puts Life into Our Faith

The Christian's faith has goodness in it only because it comes from above and is born of the Spirit. On the other hand, the Deist's infidelity is bad because it comes from below, is born of the will of the flesh and the will of men, and rejects the necessity of being saved from the corruption of fallen nature. Therefore, the Christian who rejects, reproaches, and writes against the necessity of direct, divine inspiration also advocates the whole cause of infidelity. He confirms the ground on which the infidel stands! The only proof he has for the goodness of his own Christianity is that which equally proves the goodness of the Deist's infidelity.

Without the new birth, or without direct, continual, divine inspiration, which is the same thing, there is no real difference between the Christian and the infidel. Whether the uninspired, unregenerate son of Adam is in the church or out of the church, he is still a child of this world, a fallen Adam and a mere natural man, to whom the things of the Spirit of God are foolishness. The evidence of this is obvious when we see that the same so-called virtues and the same glaring vices are common to both the infidel and the nominal Christian who does not have the life of the Spirit in him.

This nominal Christian, who does not have the Spirit of God continually inspiring and working in him, has only a Christianity of his own making. He may have the appearance of being virtuous, yet he has all the vices that his natural self wants to have. He may renounce what is called natural religion, but unless he is a newly born and divinely inspired

Christian, he will live and die in all his natural corruption.

Throughout the Scriptures, the divine life is the highest aim and intention for man. The Scriptures make it evident that only the holy, life-giving Spirit of God has the power to raise up such a life; nothing else is even so much as hinted at. How blind is the man, therefore, who cannot see these two fundamental truths while reading about the Gospel and the history of gospel Christians: that the divine life is the only source of divine knowledge in man, and that only a birth of the divine nature can bring about this divine life within him.

The Spirit Puts Life into Our Knowledge

Even so, when these truths are lost or given up, people of vain learning and a worldly spirit set up kingdoms of strife and division over the Gospel Book. For what purpose? They say it is so that the unity of the church may not be lost! But their attempts are in vain. They create more and more systems of empty notions and opinions, and for what? So that words and forms may do for the church now, what could only be done for the first church by the new birth of the Spirit.

Bible scholars are often looked upon as having divine knowledge of Scripture because so many of them can easily call to mind a chapter and verse. Also, nothing is really considered erroneous among students of the Scriptures, except for supposed mistakes in the Hebrew or Greek languages. They act like students of Milton or Shakespeare, charging one another with tiny blunders.

Now, by calling such knowledge of the Scriptures divine, we make the same mistake as claiming to know everything that John knew because we can recite his whole gospel and his epistles by heart. What a fallacy! A literal knowledge of Scripture means only that we have memorized Scripture, which is far from having a divine perception of the things spoken of in the Word of God. If memorization is all it takes to attain the highest perfection in scriptural knowledge, then even the most vicious, wicked scholar in the world may attain it.

But divine knowledge and a wicked life are so inconsistent that they are mutual death and destruction to one another. Where the one is alive, the other must be dead. Judas Iscariot was acquainted with Jesus Christ and knew all that He said and did until the time of His crucifixion. He knew what it was like to be at the Lord's table and to partake of His supper of bread and wine. However, it is even truer that he knew none of this, and he had no better knowledge of it than Pontius Pilate had. Indeed, all knowledge of Christ that is not derived from divine inspiration or the new birth, is as poor and profitless as Judas's knowledge of Jesus was. One may say to Christ, *"Hail, master"* (Matt. 26:49), but *"no man can say that Jesus is the Lord, but by the Holy Ghost"* (1 Cor. 12:3).

The natural man can have this empty, outward knowledge of the sacred Scriptures and of religious matters as easily as he can have knowledge about any other books or human affairs. Yet, when this is taken to be divine knowledge, it spreads such darkness and delusion all over Christendom that it may be considered to be no less than a general apostasy from the gospel state of divine illumination.

For the gospel state has only one light, and that is the Lamb of God; it has only one life, and that is by the Spirit of God. Whatever is not of this light and is not governed by this Spirit, no matter what you may call it, is no more a part of the gospel state, nor will it have a better end, than that which *"entereth in at the mouth* [and corrupts] *the belly"* (Matt. 15:17). When Christians look more to natural knowledge of the Scriptures than to divine knowledge of the Word of God, it is very similar to the fall of the first man from innocence and heavenly purity into an earthly state.

In the early church, the light of pagans was nothing more than darkness. The wisdom of words was nothing more than friendship with the world, which is enmity with God (James 4:4). In that new church, the Tree of Life, which grew in the midst of Paradise, took root and grew up again. But in the present church, the Tree of Life is considered the visionary food of deluded fanatics. Also, the tree of death, called the Tree of Knowledge of Good and Evil, catches the attention of both pastors and congregations; it is thought to do as much good to Christians now as it did evil to the first inhabitants of Paradise. This tree, which brought death and corruption into human nature, is now called a tree of light, and it is watered by every corrupt stream, however distant or muddy, that can be drawn to it.

Now let me ask this simple question: Does a great scholar have any more power to say to a mountain, *"Be thou removed, and be thou cast into the sea"* (Matt. 21:21), than the uneducated Christian has? If not, he is just as weak and powerless and little in the kingdom of God as the uneducated man. But if the uneducated man's faith should happen to be closer to the size of a mustard seed than the faith of the prodigious scholar, the uneducated Christian stands far above him in the kingdom of God. This is because the great scholar, with all his worldly knowledge, has not come to Christ with the pure, simple faith of a child. Let us therefore approach God with a simple and childlike faith, and He will put us high in His kingdom.

By the Spirit We Can Commune with God

The one light and the Spirit that were from all eternity, before angels or any heavenly beings were created, must to all eternity be the one light and Spirit by which angels and men can ever have any union or communion with God. Every other light is just a light by which the beasts can see and move. Every other spirit is just a spirit that gives to flesh and blood all its lusts and appetites.

The loss of the one light and Spirit of God turned an order of angels into devils. The loss of the same light and Spirit took from the divine Adam his first crown of paradisiacal glory, stripped him more naked than the beasts, and left him a prey to devils and in the jaws of eternal death. What, therefore, can have the least share of power toward man's redemption, besides the light and Spirit of God being born again in him as they were in his first glorious creation? Or what can possibly bring forth the return of his first lost birth, but solely this eternal light and Spirit?

Our Lord affirmed the gospel state to be the kingdom of heaven at hand, or the kingdom of heaven that has come among men. This kingdom has the nature of no worldly thing or creaturely power. It serves no worldly ends, can be helped by no worldly power, receives nothing from man except man's full denial of himself, and stands upon nothing that is finite or transitory. It has no existence except in the working power of God that created and upholds heaven and earth. And it is a kingdom of a God who became man, and a kingdom of men united to God, through direct and continual divine illumination.

Is there any Scripture of the New Testament that does not prove this to be the gospel state—a kingdom of God into which no one can enter unless he is born of the Spirit? The Scriptures affirm that no one can continue to be alive unless he is led by the Spirit. And no thought, desire, or action can have any part in the gospel state unless it is a fruit of the Spirit.

"Thy kingdom come. Thy will be done in earth, as it is in heaven" (Matt. 6:10). God's kingdom in heaven is the manifestation of what God is and what He does in His heavenly creatures. His will is done there because His Holy Spirit is the life, the power, and the mover of everything that lives in heaven. We may recite the Lord's Prayer every day, and yet, for the sake of "orthodoxy," we may preach and write against all that is prayed for in it. For nothing but a continual, direct, divine illumination can do what we pray will be done.

God's kingdom comes where every other power besides His is at an end and has been driven out. His will can only be done where the Spirit that wills in God also wills in the creature. Let us strive to be children of His kingdom and recipients of His power, and nothing else.

Chapter 7

Denying Oneself
before God

I f we consider the nature of our salvation, it ought
to be obvious to us that bringing secular literature into the Christian church is not going to
have a good effect upon fallen man. The wit and
style of secular authors, past and present, cannot
cause the doctrines of the Cross to increase man's
salvation in any respect. The Gospel would be poorly
preached if the wisdom of words and the gifts of human intelligence and imagination were its genuine
helps.

However, we may be sure that the Gospel is as
contrary to human wisdom as self-denial is to self-
gratification. To know the truth of gospel salvation
is to know that man's natural wisdom is to be
equally sacrificed with his natural folly. Indeed, human wisdom and human folly are one and the same
thing; sometimes they are called by the one name,
and sometimes by the other.

Because of the Fall, man's intellectual faculties
are in a far worse state than his natural animal appetites, and they require a much greater self-denial.
Everyone knows that an intense and daily study of

culinary arts will not help a believer to have the spirit and practice of Christian abstinence. Likewise, when man's own will, understanding, and imagination have their natural strength indulged and gratified; when these are made seemingly rich and honorable with the treasures acquired from a study of classic literature apart from the Scriptures, they will not help him at all to be like-minded with Christ.

In order to know all this as the truth, you need to know these two things: first, that our salvation consists wholly in being saved from ourselves, or from what we are by nature; and, secondly, that this salvation is only manifested in us by the sort of godly humility that is beyond all expression. Hence, the first unalterable condition of salvation to fallen man is this, as spoken by the one and only Savior:

> *If any man come to me, and hate not his father, and mother, and wife, and children, and brethren, and sisters, yea, and his own life also, he cannot be my disciple.*   *(Luke 14:26)*

To show that this is only the beginning of and the foundation for man's salvation, the Savior added, *"Learn of me; for I am meek and lowly in heart"* (Matt. 11:29).

The Importance of Self-Denial

What light is here for those who can bear it; what light for those who love the light! Self is the whole evil of our fallen nature, but self-denial is our capacity for being saved; humility is our savior. This is every man's short lesson of life, and anyone who learns it well has the most complete education. Then the old Adam, with all his ignorance, is cast out of him; and when Christ's humility is learned, then he has the very mind of Christ, and he may be brought forth as a son of God.

Why, then, are there so many books in libraries that have taken the place of this short lesson of the Gospel? Why have so many great disputers of the ages been up in arms to support and defend a set of opinions, doctrines, and practices that have so little of self-denial and humility?

People display great ignorance by running to various schools of thought to learn how to put off Adam and to put on Christ. Can the fountains of pagan poets and authors help us to more divinely drink of the cup that Christ drank of? What can result from all this but that which has too often been the result already—a faith colored by the ideas of someone like Cicero instead of a true belief in the Word of God? Instead of having the spirit of the humble publican, seeking to regain paradise and crying out with a broken heart, *"God be merciful to me a sinner"* (Luke 18:13), the highbred classicist will live in daily transports of joy over the high-sounding words of a writer such as Milton.

This will be more or less the case with all the salvation doctrines of Christ while they remain under the administration of worldly scholars. Divine truths have their redeeming power only when they are spirit and life (John 6:63) in us, and they can have no real birth in us unless we die to ourselves and have broken and contrite hearts. Otherwise, such truths will serve only to help people to squander the beautiful colors of salvation on paper monuments of lifeless virtue.

How did worldly scholars become so prideful and vain? How did they become so unable to come under the humility of the Cross? It was because the natural man desired to glory in his own cultivated abilities. Can a person's intelligence or elegant tastes do any more good or have any more redeeming power in Christians than in unbelievers? We might as well say that it is good for a Christian to have his own will, but it is bad and destructive for a non-Christian!

Our Redeemer said, *"Without me ye can do nothing"* (John 15:5). Whatever is not His direct work in us is, at best, nonexistent with respect to the good of our redemption. To the builders' eyes, a Tower of Babel may seem to hide its head in the clouds. However, it is no nearer to heaven than the earth on which it stands is. It is the same with all the buildings of man's wisdom and natural abilities with respect to the things of salvation. A person may take the logic and rhetoric of the best thinkers and speakers, and then ascend as high as he can on the ladder of ideas, yet he will have done no more to revive the lost life of God in his soul than if he had built the Tower of Babel himself.

Self is the root, the tree, and the branches of all the evils of our fallen state. We are without God because we are in the life of self. Self-love, self-glorying, and self-seeking are the very essence and life of pride; and the Devil, the first father of pride, is never absent from them or without power in them. To die to these things of the self is to make the Devil depart from us. But, as soon as we allow our own abilities to have a share in our good works, the satanic spirit of pride unites with us, and we begin again to maintain self-love, self-glorying, and self-seeking in our hearts.

All the vices of fallen angels and men originate with the pride of self. In other words, all our vices get their power from the atheism and idolatry of self, for self is indeed both an atheist and an idolater. It is an atheist because it has rejected God, and it is an idolater because it is its own idol. On the other hand, all the virtues of the heavenly life are the virtues of humility. There is not a joy or glory or praise in heaven that does not come out of humility. It is humility alone that can traverse the otherwise unpassable gulf between heaven and hell. Humility is the one thing that has led every angel to heaven, while pride is the fire that has led all the devils to hell.

Pride versus Humility

So then, what is the great struggle for eternal life, or in what does it lie? It all lies in the strife between pride and humility. Pride and humility are the two master powers, the two kingdoms that strive for the eternal possession of man. All other things, no matter what they may be, are like slaves under them.

Let us observe, then, that every son of Adam, if he is doing whatever he wants, is in the service of pride and self until he is redeemed by the humility that comes solely from heaven. Until then, all that he does will only be done for attention and praise. Also, anyone who thinks it is possible for the natural man to get a better humility than this from his own educated and refined reason, proves that he is quite ignorant of the plainest and most vital truth of the Gospel, namely, that there is only one true humility in the whole world, and that is the humility of Christ.

Since the fall of Adam, no man has had even the smallest degree of humility except from Christ. Humility is one in the same sense that Christ is one, the Mediator is one, and redemption is one. There are not two Lambs of God that take away the sins of the world. But if there were any humility besides that of Christ, there would be something else besides Him that could take away the sins of the world. *"All that ever came before me,"* said Christ, *"are thieves and robbers"* (John 10:8). We are used to confining this verse to people, but we can also say the same of every virtue—whether it has the name of humility, love, piety, or anything else—if it comes before Christ. However good it may appear, it is only a cheat, a thief, and a robber if it tries to take the name of godly virtue.

The reason for this is that self and pride control all of man until man gets his all from Christ. Therefore, a person may *"fight the good fight"* (1 Tim. 6:12) only if he fights against the idolatrous nature of self, so that it may be brought to its death by the supernatural humility of Christ brought to life in him.

But there are many enemies to man's rising out of the fall of Adam through the Spirit and power of Christ. The one great enemy is self-exaltation. This is the Antichrist's beginning, pomp, power, and throne. When self-exaltation ceases, the last enemy will be destroyed, and all that came from the pride and death of Adam will be swallowed up in victory (Isa. 25:8).

Many people are watching to see where and what the Antichrist is, or by what signs he may be known. Some say that he has been in the Christian world almost ever since the gospel times. They say, in fact, that he was even then beginning to appear and show himself. Others say he came into the world with this or that pope; still others say that he has not yet come, but that he will come soon. Some insist that he has been here and there, but has been driven from one place to another by several different Protestant denominations when they have arisen.

But to know with certainty where and what the Antichrist is, who is with him, and who is against him, you need only to read the short descriptions that Christ gave of Himself: *"The Son can do nothing of himself"* (John 5:19); *"I came…not to do mine own will"* (John 6:38); *"I seek not mine own glory"* (John 8:50); *"I am meek and lowly in heart"* (Matt. 11:29). Now, if this is Christ, then self-exaltation, because it is entirely contrary to all this, must be the one great antichrist that opposes and stands against the whole nature and Spirit of Christ.

The Evil of Self-Exaltation

The main things, therefore, that everyone has to fear, renounce, and abhor, are every inward exaltation of himself and every outward work that proceeds from it. But where should a man look to find self working in him—the self that raises pride to its greatest strength and most of all hinders the birth of the humble Jesus in his soul? Should he call all the vanities of the world the highest works of self-adoration? Should he look at the materialistic men and women of the world to see the pride that has the most of the antichrist in it? No, by no means. These are indeed shameful marks of the vain, foolish heart of man, but, comparatively speaking, they are only the skin-deep follies of the pride that the fall of man has brought forth in everyone.

If you want to see the deepest root and the iron strength of pride and self-adoration, you must enter into the dark chamber of man's fiery soul. When the light of God (which is the only thing that gives humility and meek submission to all created spirits) was extinguished by the death that Adam died, Satan, or self-exaltation, became the strongman that kept possession of man's soul until *"a stronger than he* [came] *upon him"* (Luke 11:22). Satan set up a kingdom of pride and vanity in the heart of man, and all outward pride and vanity became the childish, transitory playthings of such a kingdom.

The inward strongman of pride, the diabolical self, therefore, has his works within the heart of man; he dwells in the strength of the heart and has every power and faculty of the soul offering continual incense to him. His memory, his will, his understanding, and his imagination are always at work for him and for no one else. His memory is the faithful storehouse of all the fine things that self has ever done; and so that none of them are lost or forgotten, his memory is continually setting them before his mind. Though he has the whole world before him, he does not go after anything unless the self causes the will to do it. His understanding is always looking for new projects to enlarge the dominions of self; and if this fails, imagination comes in, as the last and truest support of self, and makes him a king and a mighty lord of castles in the air.

This natural self must be pulled out of the heart and totally denied, or there can be no disciple of Christ. Truly, the atheistic, self-idolatrous nature of the old man must be put off, or there can be no new creature in Christ.

Putting Off the Old Man

Now, what is in the human soul that most of all hinders the death of the old man? What, above all other things, strengthens and exalts the life of self and makes it the master and governor of all the powers of the heart and soul? It is the imagined riches of man's faculties, the glitter of genius, the flights of imagination, the glory of learning, and the self-conceited strength of natural reason. These are the strongholds of fallen nature, the master builders of pride's temple in the heart of man, and the daily worshippers of self. All these magnified talents of the natural man began with his miserable fall from the life of God in his soul.

If man had remained in the holy image of the Father, Son, and Holy Spirit, then intelligence, learning, and natural reason would never have had a name among men. Such things would have been thought of as we now think of ignorance and sickness. Everything that dwelt in man or came from man would have acknowledged God, and not man; it would have shown that the heavenly powers of the triune life of God were dwelling in him. Man would not even have thought to acknowledge his own natural intelligence or power of goodness.

But, as it is, man's dreadful fall from the life of God in his soul has furnished him with his bestial appetites and lusts. When the lusts of the flesh have been entirely spent, when earthly flesh and blood have been forced to let the soul go free, then all of man's bright talents will end with the system of fleshly lusts in which they began. Anything that remains of man will have nothing of its own, nothing that can say, "I do this," or, "I do that." Rather, all that man has or does will be either the glory of God manifested in him or the power of hell in full possession of his soul.

Many people imagine themselves to be something great in the intellectual world. Even so, the years in which men may use their faculties and abilities may be much shorter than they think. When the time comes for fine homes, riches, and honors to leave them, everything must bear full witness to Solomon's *"vanity of vanities"* (Eccl. 1:2). All the things of this world are hopeless displays of vanity.

Therefore, the well-known, accomplished scholar ought to reflect on the fact that all his faculties and abilities come from the same place as the Serpent's trickery. Also, he ought to see that he cannot raise his soul into divine knowledge through the well-exercised powers of his natural reason and imagination. He might as well dream of acquiring angelic purity by adding new delights to his natural lusts and passions!

The only intellectual power that can help to bring man again into the region of divine light, is that poor, despised thing called simplicity. Simplicity stops the workings of the fallen nature, and it leaves room for God to work again in the soul, according to the good pleasure of His holy will. It stands waiting before God, in readiness for the divine birth, just as the plants of the earth wait for the inflow of light and air. In contrast, the self-assuming works of man's natural powers shut him up in himself, thereby closing him off from the inflow of the light and Spirit of God.

In the lapsed state of the church, with its proud endowments of fallen nature, the worldly scholar often plays the critic. Weighed down with pagan wisdom and skill, he criticizes the simplicity of salvation mysteries—mysteries that point only to the inward work of the triune God in the soul of man and the raising up of a dead Adam into the life of Christ. Additionally, the well-read scholar tries to use his mind and his education to manage the doctrines of salvation, so he asserts that the ancient way of knowing the things of God is obsolete. The fishermen-apostles who taught and practiced these doctrines indeed needed to have divine knowledge from the direct, continual operation of the Holy Spirit. But this state, according to the man of the world, was only for a time—until man's genius and learning entered into the domain of the church.

If ever *"the abomination of desolation"* (Matt. 24:15) is found standing in the Holy Place, this is it! For as soon as man's natural faculties and acquired learning are said to have the right and power to guide men into the truth—which was once the office and power of the Holy Spirit—as soon as this doctrine is set up, and as far as it is received, then the kingdom of God is entirely closed off, and only a kingdom of scribes, Pharisees, and hypocrites can fill its place.

By this doctrine, the whole nature and power of gospel religion is denied. Christ has never given power to logic, learning, or the natural faculties of man in His kingdom. He has never said of Himself, "It is expedient for you that I go away, so that your own natural abilities and educated reason may guide you into all truth." We have no record of His saying this, and we cannot find such meaning in any of His words.

The Highest Kingdom

The first and main doctrine of Christ and His apostles was to tell the Jews, and then the rest of the world, that the kingdom of God was at hand, or that it had come to them (Matt. 4:17). Surely this was proof enough that the Jewish nation was not the kingdom of God, even though it had been appointed by God and was under His laws. Why was the Jewish nation not the kingdom of God, when it had been set up by God? Because it had human and worldly things in it; it consisted of carnal ordinances, and it had only the shadows of the kingdom of God that was to come. Christ said, *"My kingdom is not of this world"* (John 18:36). To prove it, He added, *"If my kingdom were of this world, then would my servants fight, that I should not be delivered to the Jews"* (v. 36).

Jesus was saying that God's kingdom is so different from and so superior to this world, that no worldly power could either help or hinder it. This is the truth of the kingdom of God that has come unto men. The birthright privilege of all who are living members of it, is deliverance from the nature that they received from Adam, from the spirit and wisdom of this world. Through the whole course of their lives, they may now say and do and be all that the Spirit of their Father works in them.

But now, if we are left again to our own natural powers, to run here and there looking for God's kingdom instead of allowing the Spirit to speak, do, and work everything in us and for us, has this kingdom not gone away from us, and are we not left comfortless? Would it not have been better for us to have been still under the law, sacrificing bulls and goats, than to be brought under a religion that is determined by the wisdom and carnality of this world? Indeed, where the Spirit of God is not the direct, continual governor of spiritual things, nothing good can come of it. But where He is the overseer, only good can arise.

Chapter 8

The Keys to
Knowing God

What is the difference between man's own righteousness and man's own knowledge in religion? There is no difference. They are exactly the same thing, and they do the same work, namely, to keep up and strengthen every evil, vanity, and corruption of fallen nature. The only thing that can save a man from his own righteousness is that which can save and deliver him from his own knowledge. Recall the story of the rich young ruler. He was in the greatest opposition to the Gospel, and he had the hardest time receiving it, because he trusted in his own righteousness. It was *"easier for a camel to go through the eye of a needle"* (Matt. 19:24) than for him to enter the kingdom of God. But keep in mind that the Christian who trusts in his own light is the same as the Jew who trusted in his own righteousness.

Why has the Spirit of God given the false church such names as a beast, a scarlet whore, a horned dragon, and other horrible descriptions of diabolical power (Rev. 17:3–5)? Why has the Spirit described the nominal church as driven into a wilderness (Rev.

12:6)? Why have the two faithful witnesses, Moses and Jesus, been portrayed as prophesying for so many ages in sackcloth, and slain in the streets of spiritual Sodom and Egypt (Rev. 11:3, 7–8)? Because man's natural wisdom, man's own conceited righteousness, his serpentine wickedness, his self-love, his sensual spirit and worldly power, have seized the mysteries of salvation and built them up into a kingdom of envious strife and contention.

This is the beast, the whore, and the dragon that has governed and will govern every private Christian and every public church body until, dead to all that is self, they turn to God—not to a God that they have only heard of with their ears, but to a God of life, light, and power, found living and working within them as the essential life, light, and power of their own lives. For God is only our God when His own divine nature is birthed within us. This, and nothing but this, is our whole relationship to Him, our whole fellowship with Him, our whole knowledge of Him, and our whole capacity of having any part in the mysteries of gospel salvation.

Who can seek the kingdom of God or hunger and thirst after His righteousness? Who can cry, *"Abba, Father"* (Gal. 4:6)? Who can pray, *"Thy kingdom come"* (Matt. 6:10)? Who can say of Christ, *"My Lord and my God"* (John 20:28)? Only the person who is born of God and has the divine nature in him. Only God in man can bring about a godly life in man.

Scripture by Itself Is Death

This is why the apostle wrote, *"The letter killeth, but the spirit giveth life"* (2 Cor. 3:6). But perhaps you will say, "Can this be true of the divine letter of the Gospel? Can it really kill?" Yes, it can kill when it is rested in, when it is seen as divine power, and when it is thought to have goodness in itself. In this way, the letter of the Gospel kills the Spirit of God in us because it quenches His holy fire within us and replaces His power in us. The letter of Scripture brings death when it is built into systems of strife and contention about words, ideas, and opinions, and when it causes the kingdom of God to consist of mere words rather than of power. (See 1 Corinthians 4:20.) When it is used in this manner, it cannot do anything but kill, because it keeps people from the only thing that is life and can give life.

This, then, is the whole of the matter: all the truths and doctrines and expressions of the written Word have only one nature and one purpose: they all say to man what Christ said when He beckoned, *"Come unto me, all ye that labour and are heavy laden, and I will give you rest"* (Matt. 11:28). *"Christ Jesus, who of God is made unto us wisdom, and righteousness, and sanctification"* (1 Cor. 1:30), is our only refreshment. He is our life source: *"As the branch cannot bear fruit of itself, except it abide in the vine; no more can ye, except ye abide in me....Without me ye can do nothing"* (John 15:4–5).

Therefore, to come to Christ, to have our fallen natures refreshed by Him, to be born of His Spirit, to have His heavenly flesh and heavenly blood made alive in us before we put off this body and blood of death that we have from Adam, is the only thing meant by all that the Scriptures say of the merits and benefits of having Christ. The Spirit, the body, the blood of Christ within us are our whole peace with God, our whole adoption, our whole redemption, our whole justification, our whole glorification. This is the one meaning of that new birth of which Christ said, *"Except a man be born* [again from above], *he cannot enter into the kingdom of God"* (John 3:5).

All that is said about Christ in the Scriptures, though the expressions may vary greatly, has only one meaning and points to only one thing. Why is this? Because the whole state and nature of fallen man lacks only one thing, which is a real rebirth of the divine nature in him. When the divine nature is born again in us, all that can be done for our salvation is done. The Law, the Prophets, and the Gospel are fulfilled when a new creature is in Christ, having his life in and from Him, just as the branch has its life in and from the vine.

When all Scripture is thus understood; when all that Christ said of Himself and all that His apostles said of Him is heard or read as a call to come to Christ; when we come to Him in hunger and thirst to be filled and blessed with His divine nature made alive within us; then, and only then, the letter does not kill, but like a sure guide leads directly to life. But when those who know nothing about Scripture except its words try to dissect it with the tools of grammar, logic, and criticism, they bring forth nothing but their own wisdom of words, and a religion of bickering, hatred, and contention.

As lamentable as this is, there is something worse. For a long time, the letter of Scripture has been the so-called property of critics and well-educated thinkers, who have used it almost as a commodity. As a result, the difference between literal

knowledge and living, divine knowledge is almost
lost in the Christian world. The moment a person
thinks that more must be known about God, about
Christ, and about the powers of the world to come,
than every scholar can know by reading the letter of
Scripture, he is immediately called a fanatic, even if
he is a leader in the church. There would be some
excuse for this if these critics could first prove that
the apostle's text should be read, "The spirit killeth,
but the letter giveth life." But as it is, there is no
excuse for such accusations.

Something Missing in the Church

The real difference between literal and divine
knowledge is set forth in the highest degree of clarity in these words of our Savior: *"The kingdom of
heaven is like unto treasure hid in a field"* (Matt.
13:44). After reading the whole parable, we see that
the true benefit and power of the letter of Scripture
is that it tells us about a treasure that we need, a
treasure that belongs to us, and how and where it is
to be found. Verse forty-four continues by saying
that when a man *"goeth and selleth all that he hath,
and buyeth that field,"* then divine knowledge begins
in him. This is nothing else but the treasure possessed and enjoyed.

Now, this is the same thing that Christ meant
when He said, essentially, "Unless a man denies
himself and forsakes all that he has, he cannot be
My disciple." (See Luke 14:26–27.) In other words,
Christ was saying, "Man cannot partake of My mind,
My Spirit, and My nature, and therefore cannot
know Me, unless he denies himself. He will only hear

about the treasure unless he enters into the possession and enjoyment of it." And so it is with all Scripture. The letter of Scripture can only direct a person to doing what it cannot do itself, and it can only give notice of something that it cannot give.

Of course, there is a clear and evident distinction between the instruction to do something and the real participation in it. However, the majority of Christians seem to form all their religious perceptions and all their knowledge of divine things from the literal words of Scripture, without being aware of anything else. People know about good and evil, but the mere knowledge of good and evil has no effect upon such powers in their lives. Even so, the only knowledge that is thought to be of any value in these times is that which is merely the work of the brain.

Thus, as soon as a man of thought can explain what he calls the being and attributes of God, he thinks, and others think, that he truly knows God. But what excuse can be made for such foolishness, when Scripture has plainly told him that to know God is eternal life? To know God is to have the power, the life, and the Spirit of God manifested in one's life, and therefore it is eternal life. *"No man knoweth...the Father, save the Son, and he to whomsoever the Son will reveal him"* (Matt. 11:27). The revelation of the Son is the birth of the Son in the soul; and only a new creature in Christ has knowledge of God—what He is and does and works in the soul.

What Faith Really Is

Suppose that an individual, while reading the letter of Scripture, immediately thinks that he knows what faith is and that he is in the faith. Sad delusion! For to know what faith is, or to know that we are in the faith, is to know that Christ is truly in us; it is to know in our souls the power of His life, His sufferings, His death, His resurrection, and His ascension. To be in the faith is to rid ourselves of all ideas and opinions about it, because faith is only found and felt by its living power and fruits within us, which are righteousness, peace, and joy in the Holy Spirit. These three things can only be found in Jesus Christ, who is our righteousness, our peace, and our joy. They cannot be found by merely reading the Scriptures.

Therefore, faith is not in us because of any opinion we may have, but it is Christ, or the divine nature, in us. If it were otherwise, the operation of faith in us could not lead us to righteousness, peace, and joy in the Holy Spirit. *"By grace are ye saved through faith"* (Eph. 2:8) means only, "You are saved by Christ." If faith were anything else but Christ or a birth of the divine nature within us, it could do us no good; no power could be ascribed to it; it could not be our victory; it could not overcome the world, the flesh, and the Devil. Every faith that is not Christ in us is a dead faith.

How trifling, therefore, to look for some difference between faith and its works, between a justification by faith and justification by its works. Is there any difference between Christ as a redeemer, and His redeeming works? Can one be set above the other in its effectiveness to redeem? If not, then faith and its works, which are Christ in us, can have no separation from, or excellence above, one another. Rather, they are one, just as Christ is one, just as our Savior and our salvation are one in us.

Everything that has been said of faith, from the Garden of Eden until now, has only been said about the power and life of a redeeming Christ working within us. Therefore, to divide faith from its works is as absurd as dividing a circle from its roundness. There would be no salvation by faith if it were not Christ Himself, the power of God, living and working in us. If faith were not Christ within us— without whom we can do nothing (John 15:5)—no one would ever have said that every power of the world, the flesh, and the Devil must yield to faith.

Without Christ we can do nothing, and yet all things are possible to our faith. Do we need any more proof that our faith is nothing else but Christ born and living within us? Whatever power within us leads us to salvation—whether it is faith or hope or prayer or hunger after the kingdom of God and His righteousness—it is all one power, and that one power is Christ within us. Therefore, if faith and its good works are Christ living in us, any distinction that we try to make between faith and its works is mere ignorant jargon, just as it would be if we tried to make a distinction between life and its living operations.

When the church, the kingdom of God among men, was first set up, the apostle Paul boasted that all other wisdom or learning had sunk into nothing. *"Where,"* he said, *"is the wise? where is the scribe? where is the disputer of this world? hath not God made foolish the wisdom of this world?"* (1 Cor. 1:20). But now, churches boast that they are full of wise men who have even more knowledge than Paul had, and have the mysteries of the kingdom of God committed to them. Is it any surprise, then, that out of a religion of heavenly love, built upon the redeeming life and doctrine of a Son of God dying to save the whole world, division, bitterness, envy, pride, strife, hatred, and persecution have broken forth with more strength in learned Christendom than they ever did from a religion of pagan idolatry set up by Satan?

Love, the Key to True Knowledge

With this, one might ask, Must there then be no learning, no knowledge in the Christian church? Is the Gospel to spur no thought and to provide nothing but mere salvation? Must the ministers of the Gospel know nothing and teach nothing but the full denial of self, poverty of spirit, meekness, humility, unwearied patience, unceasing love, absolute renunciation of the vanities of the world, and full dependence upon our heavenly Father? Must there be no joy or rejoicing but in the Holy Spirit; no wisdom but that which God gives; no walking but as Christ walked; no reward or glory for our labors of love but that of being found in Christ?

To this the first answer is, Only those who hunger after nothing but the Bread of Life who came down from heaven, acknowledging no master but Christ, no teacher but His Holy Spirit, can be happy. Ministers who seek only to be taught by God, and who seek the same for others, will have the joy of the Lord.

Secondly, everything that I have written here so far is only intended to promote knowledge in the Christian church, so that all ignorance and darkness may be driven out of it. The church of Christ is the school of all the highest knowledge that human nature is capable of in this life. Ignorance is everywhere except in the church of Christ. The Law, the Prophets, and the Gospel are the only treasures that can be called the knowledge of God and man. The person in whom the Law, the Prophets, and the Gospel are fulfilled is the only well-educated man, and one of the first-rate scholars in the world.

But now, who possesses the wisdom of these rich treasures? In whom is everything taught by the Scriptures known and fulfilled? The lips of truth have told us that it is he, and he alone, who loves God *"with all the heart, and with all the understanding, and with all the soul, and with all the strength, and...his neighbour as himself"* (Mark 12:33). This is the man who is filled with wisdom and light, and has been led into the full possession of all the mysteries contained in the Law, the Prophets, and the Gospel.

Where this divine love is lacking, a diabolical self sits in its place. You may be a great thinker, a shining critic, a moving speaker, a poet, or a profound philosopher, but if you want to know the mysteries of nature, the reasons for good and evil in this world, the relationship between the visible and invisible world, or how the things of time proceed from and are influenced by the powers of eternity, there is only one key of entrance. The only thing that can open the vision is love, the same love that began and carries on everything that works in both the spiritual and the physical realms. Recall how Paul said, *"Though I have the gift of prophecy, and understand all mysteries, and all knowledge; and though I have all faith, so that I could remove mountains, and have not* [love], *I am nothing"* (1 Cor. 13:2). Love is absolutely essential.

If you wish to know the mysteries of grace and salvation, if you wish to go forth as a faithful witness of gospel truths, wait until this fire of divine love has had its perfect work in you. For until your heart is an altar on which this heavenly fire never goes out, you are dead in yourself and can only speak dead words about things that never had any life within you. Without a real birth of this divine love in the essence of your being, no matter how well educated you are, your heart is but the dark heart of fallen Adam, and your knowledge of the kingdom of God will be the knowledge of the murderer Cain. Everything is murder without love.

If love is not the breath of your life, the spirit that forms and governs everything that proceeds from you, and the essence of everything that you do and agree to, then you are broken off from the works of God. Without love, you are without God, and your name, nature, and works can have no other name but pride, wrath, envy, hypocrisy, hatred, revenge, and self-exaltation—all of which lie under the power of Satan in his kingdom of darkness. The only thing that can possibly save you from being the certain prey of all these evil spirits, through the whole course of your life, is a birth of the love that is God Himself—His light and His Spirit within you.

Because He First Loved Us

There is no knowledge in heaven besides what proceeds from this birth of love, and there is no difference between the highest light of an angel and the horrid darkness of a devil except the difference that love has made. But now, since divine love can have no beginning in us unless there is a rebirth of the divine nature in us, we say, *"We love him, because he first loved us"* (1 John 4:19). This is the same as saying that we desire God because He first desired us. We could not desire God if He had not first desired us, and we could not turn to Him if He had not first turned to us.

And so it is that we could not love God unless He first loved us. That is, we could not love Him unless He first brought forth and continued the birth of His Spirit of love in us—brought it forth by our creation and continued it by our redemption. His Holy Spirit must first be a gift to us, or born in us, and then we may worship God in spirit. In the same way, His love must be a gift to us, or born in us, and then we may have the quality of God in us that can love Him with His own love. Truly, *"love is of God; and every one that loveth is born of God"* (1 John 4:7).

This is my excuse to the educated world for acknowledging only the school of wisdom in which the lesson is divine love and the teacher is the Spirit of God. This is neither wild nor radical; it is no wilder than acknowledging only one God. All the wisdom and learning of scholars, in any other school but this, will provide no comfort at the hour of death. Until a man is thoroughly convinced of this, he ought to find enough proof in the fact that he is not yet in the light of truth, not yet taught by God, and not yet like-minded with Christ.

One of Christ's followers said, *"Lord, suffer me first to go and bury my father"* (Matt. 8:21). Jesus answered, *"Follow me; and let the dead bury their dead"* (v. 22). Another said to him, *"Let me first go bid them farewell, which are at home at my house"* (Luke 9:61). Jesus answered, *"No man, having put his hand to the plow, and looking back, is fit for the kingdom of God"* (v. 62). Now, suppose that a third individual had said, "Lord, I have left several books at home, written by the greatest masters of grammar, logic, and eloquence. Allow me first to go back for them, lest I lose the light that I had from them, and mistake the depth and truth of Your heavenly doctrines."

How absurd is this last request! And yet, scholars and critics of divinity are saying exactly the same thing! They do not look to Christ alone, as He has taught us to do. Rather, they look to their own wisdom, their own knowledge, and the literal words of Scripture, all of which lack life without the love and Spirit of our Lord.

Chapter 9

The One
Essential Thing

The Lord Jesus said, *"I am the light of the world: he that followeth me shall not walk in darkness"* (John 8:12). Spiritual light and spiritual darkness are as separate from one another as the light and darkness of this world were on the first day of Creation. Jesus Christ, the eternal Son of God, is the only light of both men and angels. Everything about fallen nature—the selfish and prideful will, the highest abilities, natural wisdom, cleverness, and cunning—is simply the fullness of spiritual darkness, from which nothing but works of darkness can come forth. Simply put, darkness is the whole natural man, and light is the man born anew from above. Christ said, *"I am the light of the world,"* because He alone is the birth of heaven in the fallen souls of men.

But now, he who seeks to have his mind enriched and to have his fallen soul cultivated by the literature of poets, novelists, philosophers, skeptics, and critics, rejects this divine light and chooses darkness instead. This is like going to the serpent to be taught the innocent spirit of the dove, or to lustful

107

men to learn purity of heart and to kindle the flame of heavenly love in our souls! This is the very same wisdom of those who go to pagan teachers to learn how to work in Christ's vineyard. Surely those who turn to human wisdom do not savor the things that are of God; they do not walk in the light of Christ, and they are not led by the Spirit of God.

The Fire and Spirit of Heaven

What foolishness it is to expect to excel in divine knowledge through meditating on the thoughts and writings of natural men! Read what John the Baptist said about Christ:

> *I indeed baptize you with water unto repentance:*
> *but he that cometh after me is mightier than I,*
> *whose shoes I am not worthy to bear: he shall*
> *baptize you with the Holy Ghost, and with fire.*
> *(Matt. 3:11)*

Now, if what John the Baptist said is not our faith, if we do not receive it as the truth in which we are to stand firmly, then, no matter how educated we may be, we have no better a faith and no higher a wisdom than those blind men who would not receive the testimony of John. A fire and Spirit from above was the news that he proclaimed to the world; this, and nothing else, was the kingdom of God that was at hand.

If this fire and Spirit from above have not baptized us into a birth of the life of God in our souls, then we have not found the Christ and the kingdom of God to which John bore witness. And, what is worse, if we are so bewitched by the sorcery of learning that we turn writers and preachers against this inward, redeeming fire and this heavenly Spirit, then we have the spirit of those to whom our Lord said,

Woe unto you, scribes and Pharisees, hypocrites! for ye shut up the kingdom of heaven against men: for ye neither go in yourselves, neither suffer ye them that are entering to go in.

(Matt. 23:13)

Indeed, when Adam fell under the power of sin and Satan, that heavenly fire and Spirit were extinguished, and his first union with God and all heavenly beings was brought to an end. Now, if you insist that Adam did not have this heavenly fire and Spirit in the first place, or that only the fire and spirit of earthly animals lived within him, then your religion is like that of the Sadducees, who rejected the Resurrection and the existence of angels. If you deny the truth that a fullness of divine life was in the first man, then his fall and redemption are equally empty. For what can he have fallen from, or be redeemed to, if he has all the fire and spirit of life now that he ever had?

Why did John the Baptist, that burning and shining light, come and baptize with water if man was not in need of such a thing? Why did the Son of God come with His baptism by fire if man could not receive a higher fire of life than what he already had in common with the beasts of the field? Why is there all this commotion about religion and atonement? Why are there so many priestly ordinations, consecrations, churches, sacraments, and prayers? If the fire and spirit of this world are the one life and the highest life of both man and beast, then we have life on the same terms as the beasts have it, and we can only lose our lives, as they do, when we die.

However, only the fire and Spirit from heaven can cause heavenly and earthly creatures to be children of a heavenly Father. The Son of God took our human nature upon Himself and died for our sins, so that the original heavenly fire and Spirit might again come to life in us. Divine life, divine light, and divine goodness can only be kindled in our souls when the divine fire and Spirit are reborn in us. New creatures in Christ can only be taught the things of God by the Teacher from whom all the angels and principalities of heaven have their light and glory. Those who bow to the ideas and theories of natural men are therefore missing their call to have the divine life resurrected within their souls, for educated men are no different from the lowest of all other corrupt men. Remember, the Serpent differed from his fellow animals only by being more cunning than all the beasts of the field (Gen. 3:1).

Are you aware of the state of your soul? If you refuse the faith, the hope, and the desire for the heavenly fire to be kindled in your soul, then you have a religion that rejects the holy fire of God. Christ wants to kindle an unceasing, inward, celestial fire in the living temples of His children when they are born anew from above.

How, then, can we complain about atheists, infidels, and other open enemies of the gospel kingdom of God, if we reject the heavenly fire and Spirit as fanaticism and madness? We are doing the same work within the church that the atheists and infidels are doing outside of it, so we cannot rightly complain.

And if we fear having our earthly reason taken away
by the divine life of faith, then we will have neither a
higher regeneration nor the birth of God in our
souls. For this is a truth from God: until the heavenly fire and Spirit have a fullness of birth within
us, even the highest learning cannot make us any
more than eloquent speakers about the words of
Scripture.

A Kingdom Within

"The kingdom of God is within you" (Luke
17:21), said Christ. In other words, the heavenly fire
and Spirit, which are the true kingdom and manifestation of God, are within you. Where else could they
be? Even so, many people try very hard to remove
the literal meaning from these words, claiming them
to be too radical for educated minds and ears.

If you were to say, out of reverence for worldly
literature and out of abhorrence of fanaticism, that
the kingdom of God is not really within anyone, then
you would be saying that all followers of Christ are
actually dead to the kingdom of heaven. If you insist
that the heavenly fire, light, and Spirit should never
be born in an earnest, right-minded follower of
Christ, you would have a good disciple of Christ who
is as dead to the kingdom of heaven as a corpse is
dead to the outside world.

How can anyone preach the necessity of being
living members of the kingdom of heaven, and at the
same time the necessity of steadfastly believing that
a heavenly birth can never be within us? For if the
new birth can truly be within us, then it cannot be
foolish to believe that Christ spoke the truth when

He said, *"Except a man be born again* [from above], *he cannot see the kingdom of God....Except a man be born...of the Spirit, he cannot enter into the kingdom of God"* (John 3:3, 5). In other words, man cannot possibly have any godlike or divine goodness; he cannot be a child of a heavenly Father, unless he has the nature and Spirit of his heavenly Father born again in him.

All that we have in us apart from this divine birth is the fallen nature of Adam and a birth of sin, the flesh, and the Devil. The power of this heavenly birth is all the power of goodness that can ever be in a son of Adam. However, critics everywhere have tried to prove this new birth to be mere fanaticism and spiritual frenzy. Is it any wonder, therefore, that foolish doctrines, wickedness of life, lusts of the flesh, profaneness of spirit, wantonness of the mind, and contempt of goodness, all seem to be fully established among us?

Is it any wonder that sacraments, prayers, and sermons leave both men and women, both pastors and people, both the educated and the uneducated, completely unaltered in all their age-old vices? Where the one and only fountain of life and goodness is forsaken, where the seed of the divine birth is not alive and going forward, there are no differences among men with respect to the kingdom of God. It does not matter what name a person is called by, whether he is known as a zealous churchgoer, a stiff-necked Jew, a polite, civilized heathen, or a grave infidel; under all these names, the unregenerate man still has the same nature. The only differences among the unregenerate are the differences that time, place, education, appearance, hypocrisy, and

112

worldly wisdom happen to make in them. To such people, no matter what their professed religion is, the Gospel is only another book, and all that is within it will only condemn them one day.

Corruption in the Church

It ought to be obvious to everyone that the church presently stands in the kind of apostasy or fallen state that I have been describing. The whole church is in a fallen state because it has turned away from the Holy Spirit, who was promised and was given to be the only power, life, and fulfillment of all that was outwardly taught and prescribed by the Gospel. The Jews are also in a fallen state because they have refused Him who was and is the truth, the substance, the life, and the fulfillment of all that was taught and prescribed in the Law and the Prophets. Indeed, the Holy Spirit was the fulfillment of the whole Gospel just as Christ was the fulfillment of the Law.

The Holy Spirit is to be the Christian's only light, guide, and governor. Unless the Holy Spirit in man is the living reader, the living rememberer, and the living doer of the Scriptures, all that is written in the Gospel is just dead words. Therefore, where the Holy Spirit is not acknowledged and received as the whole power and life of the gospel state, it is no wonder that Christians have so few gospel virtues. If the New Testament ended without the coming of the Holy Spirit with fullness of power over sin and hell and the Devil, it would be as terrible as the Old Testament ending without the coming of a Messiah.

Do I need to write any more in order to demonstrate the truth that the one absolutely essential thing is that the Spirit of God be brought again to His first power of life in us? This was the glory of man's creation, and this alone can be the glory of his redemption. Anything besides this, anything else that passes between God and man, no matter what it may be, only reminds us of our distance from God. If we think that God is calling us by various outward dispensations, by human institutions, and so on, it is only proof that we are not yet in our true state of union with God that was intended by our redemption.

God said to Moses, *"Put off thy shoes from off thy feet, for the place whereon thou standest is holy ground"* (Exod. 3:5). Now, what God said to Moses is exactly the same thing that circumcision, the law, sacrifices, and sacraments say to man. In themselves, they are only outward signs of inward impurity and lost holiness, and they can do no more in themselves than intimate, point to, and direct us toward an inward life and new birth from above.

Mistaking the Outward for the Inward

But here lies the great mistake, or rather the idolatrous abuse, of all God's outward dispensations. They are taken to be the thing itself, to be the truth and essence of religion. What the educated Jews did with the outward letter of their Law, Christians do with the outward letter of their Gospel. Why did the Jews so furiously and obstinately cry out against Christ, *"Let him be crucified"* (Matt. 27:22)? Because their letter-learned ears, their worldly spirits, and their temple orthodoxy could not bear to hear of an inward Savior, of being born again by His Spirit, of eating His flesh and drinking His blood, of His dwelling in them and they in Him. To have their ordinances and their temple vanities engulfed by such a fulfilling Savior as this, was such fanatical jargon to their ears that they called Christ *"Beelzebub* [Satan]*"* (Matt. 10:25) and said that His doctrine was blasphemy, all for the sake of Moses and rabbinical tradition.

Do we have to ask whether the true Christ of the Gospel is less blasphemed or less crucified today? Some modern Christian theology rejects an inward Christ, a Savior living and working in the soul as its inward light and life. Do we need to ask whether a system that rejects Christ as pure madness—though His own nature and Spirit in man's soul is its only redemption—is not the same system that said of Christ when He was teaching these very things, *"He...is mad; why hear ye him"* (John 10:20)?

In a parable, our Lord portrayed the blindness of the Jews when they said of Him, *"We will not have this man to reign over us"* (Luke 19:14). Similarly, the Christian scholar, who claims to have none of this Jewish blindness, says of Christ, "We will not have this man to reign in us," and so he keeps clear of the "madness" that Paul fell into when he enthusiastically said, *"Yet not I, but Christ liveth in me"* (Gal. 2:20). Paul also said, *"Wherein thou judgest another, thou condemnest thyself; for thou that judgest doest the same things"* (Rom. 2:1). Paul's words are remarkably verified by the actions and accusations of Christians today—Christians against Jews, Christians against fellow Christians, and so on.

If we take away everything about Christ that one could call fanaticism; if we suppose that Christ cannot be a new life and Spirit within us, but only an outward, separate, distant heavenly prince; if we say that He can no more be really in us than the steeples of our churches can be in the heavens; if we insist that Christ can only live in us if an invisible hand from heaven somehow raises up great scholars or great temporal powers to be a rock in every nation for His church to stand upon; if we suppose all this (which is the very heart of modern studies of divinity), then we have a very outward Christ and a very outward kingdom, which is what the ancient Jews had dreamed of. The spiritual Christ was nailed to the cross for the sake of this outward kingdom, and He is still crucified by everyone in the church today who shares the attitudes of the Jews who wanted a temporal, earthly kingdom.

The Cause of Spiritual Blindness

Now, what is the one thing that has defeated all the gracious plans of God for fallen mankind? It is spiritual blindness. Look at the origin of the first sin, and you will see where this blindness of the heart began. If Eve had desired no other knowledge than what came from God, Paradise would have been the habitation of her and all her descendants. In the same way, after Paradise was lost, if the Jews and Christians had desired no knowledge besides what came from God, the Law and the Prophets would have kept the Jews close to the Tree of Life, and the Christian church would have been a kingdom of God and a communion of believers to this day.

However, as it happens, corruption, sin, death, and every evil of the world have entered into the church, the spouse of Christ, just as they entered into Eve, the spouse of Adam in Paradise. Such evils came in the same way and from the same cause, which was a desire for more knowledge—knowledge other than that which comes from God alone. This desire is the Devil's voice within every man, and it does everything to man now that the Serpent did to Eve then.

The Devil carries on his first deceit by tempting man with the same beautiful tree of his own will, his own mind, and his own wisdom springing up within him. This is the tree that Eve was tempted by in the Garden. This love of wisdom is so blind that it does not see that eating its fruit is exactly the same as eating the forbidden fruit. This is why men continue in the same death and separation from God that the first hunger for knowledge brought forth.

As a result, those who eagerly peruse worldly books and literature for spiritual wisdom must be told that to desire to be wise in the things of God — and to be proud of that wisdom—causes them to be grossly ignorant of those very things. This is nothing else but Eve's old Serpent and Eve's evil birth within them, and it does no better work in the church of Christ than her thirst after wisdom did in Paradise. *"Speak, LORD; for thy servant heareth"* (1 Sam. 3:9) is the only way by which any man ever did or ever can attain divine knowledge and divine goodness. To knock at any other door but this, is like asking life to come from what is dead, or like begging someone for bread when he has nothing but stones to give.

As strange as all this may seem to someone who has worked hard to learn everything that men have written in books, it is no different from what Christ said in these words: *"Except ye be converted, and become as little children, ye shall not enter into the kingdom of heaven"* (Matt. 18:3). For if critics and logicians can show that they have humbled themselves to become children of the kingdom of God by raising themselves high in their attainments, then it also may be said that he who is laboring, scheming, and fighting for all the riches he can get is the very man who has left everything behind to follow Christ, the very man who *"labour*[s] *not for the meat which perisheth"* (John 6:27).

You Have to Love God to Know Him

Show me a man whose only desire is to love God with his whole soul and spirit, and his neighbor as himself, and then you have shown me the man who knows Christ and is known by Him. He is the best and wisest man in the world, for the wisdom and goodness of the first Paradise have come to live in him. Every single precept in the Gospel is a precept of his own heart, and the joy of that newly born heavenly love is the life and light of his soul.

In this man, all that came from the old Serpent is trodden under his feet. Not a spark of self, pride, wrath, envy, covetousness, or worldly wisdom has a place in him, because the love that fulfills the whole Law and the Prophets—the love that is God and Christ, both in angels and in men—is the love that gives birth and life and growth to every thought, word, and action in him. And if he takes no part in foolish errors, if he cannot be tossed about by every wind of doctrine, it is because he is always governed by this love, which is the same as being always taught by God. On the other hand, show me a scholar as full of learning as the Vatican is of books, and he will be just as likely as the richest man in the world to give all that he has for the gospel pearl. (See Matthew 13:45–46.) In other words, he will not be very eager at all to give up his learning!

I hope you do not think that I am writing against all human literature, arts, and sciences, or that I wish the world to be without them. I am no more an enemy of them than of the common, useful activities of life. Rather, I am against the foolishness of contending about the things of God. Such strife over the literal meaning of the Scriptures can only bring harm to true Christianity. In this, I think I have all of learned Christendom on my side. For both Catholics and Protestants accuse each other of having derived a false understanding of the Gospel through their learning and logic.

Therefore, one cannot say that it is only the illiterate who condemn human wisdom in the kingdom of God. For when someone condemns the blindness of Catholic logic and criticism, he has the entire Protestant world with him. When he lays the same charge against Protestant learning, he has all the Catholic scholars logically and learnedly affirming the same thing. Thus, anyone who accuses human learning of bringing harm to the church, is far from being a fanatic; instead, he is supported by all the church learning that is in the world.

In another respect, every educated Christian agrees that temporal power in the church is hurtful to the very being and progress of a salvation kingdom that is not of this world. It is true that human power can only support and help to advance human things. And yet, the individual who claims that Christ is the one and only head, heart, and life of the church, and that *"no man can say that Jesus is the Lord, but by the Holy Ghost"* (1 Cor. 12:3), is considered to be a deranged fanatic.

How Corruption Came into the Church

Is it not high time that we look for a better foundation to stand upon than this so-called wisdom and learning? No matter where you look, you will not find any divine wisdom, knowledge, goodness, or deliverance from sin for fallen man except in these two points: first, a total entrance into the whole life of Christ; and, secondly, a total yieldedness to and dependence upon the continual operation of the Holy Spirit. We must see the Spirit as our never ceasing light, teacher, and guide into all the ways of virtue in which Christ Himself walked when He was on earth. Everything else besides this is dead work, a vain labor of the old man to create himself anew.

I want to make it clear that the only thing taught by this doctrine is a total dying to self (called the cross of Christ), so that a new creature (called Christ in us, or the Spirit of Christ come to dwell in our spirits) may be begotten in the purity and perfection of the first man's union with God. Now, if Christians forget or depart from this one divine way of salvation, if anything else but the cross of Christ and the Spirit of Christ is trusted, then all that can come from all the preachers, prayers, and sacraments is a kingdom of pagan vices. To this melancholy truth, all Christians can bear full witness. Who needs to be told that every corruption or depravity of human nature; every kind of pride, wrath, envy, malice, and self-love; every sort of hypocrisy, falseness, cursing, swearing, perjury, and cheating; every kind of wantonness, lust, and debauchery, is as common among Christians as it is among the heathen? No one wants to hear it, but everyone seems to know it is true.

Chapter 10

The New Birth
and the Church

In these last ages of Christianity, many reformations and revivals have taken place. Even so, in all their variety, they have been like so many Babels from the same Babylon. In other words, they have been like children of the same mother of confusion. Indeed, among all the reformers, the one true reformation has never yet been thought of. All that has been attempted so far is small changes in the opinions and leadership of the church, together with new role models. No one has thought to put aside worldly wisdom and to concentrate on the full leading of the Spirit of God.

The wisdom of this world is the thing that has overcome the church and carried it into captivity. No false doctrine or corrupt practice has ever prevailed without coming directly from the spirit of worldly wisdom. This wisdom is the great, evil root that should have been cut by reformation, and until this evil root is cut, the church cannot be the virgin spouse of Christ that it was at the beginning. *"If any man among you,"* said Paul, *"seemeth to be wise in this world, let him become a fool, that he may be wise"* (1 Cor. 3:18). This allows for no exception; it is a maxim as universal and unalterable as that which says, *"If any man will* [follow Christ], *let him deny himself"* (Matt. 16:24).

Man's greatest obstacle to following Christ is what the wisdom and spirit of this world do in him. *"For all that is in the world, the lust of the flesh, and the lust of the eyes, and the pride of life"* (1 John 2:16), are the very things in which the wisdom of this world lives and moves and has its being. Such wisdom can rise no higher, nor be any better, than such lusts and pride. Heavenly wisdom is the sum total of all heavenly goodness, and earthly wisdom is the whole evil of all earthly nature.

Paul spoke of a *"natural man"* (1 Cor. 2:14), who cannot know the things of God because to him they are mere foolishness. This natural man is only another name for the wisdom of this world; he cannot know the things of God, yet he can know their names and learn to speak just as the saints of God speak about them. He can claim to believe them, can eloquently praise them, and can set them forth in such a desirable manner that the children of worldly wisdom will find them quite agreeable. This is the natural man who, having gotten into the church and church power, has turned the things of God into things of this world.

If this sort of person had been kept out of the church, the church would have kept its first purity to this day, and it would not have fallen into the hands of the natural man of this world. Yet, because the church is in this fallen state, the wisdom of this world (which always loves its own) is in love with it, spares no cost to maintain it, makes laws and fights battles in defense of it, and condemns every man as heretical who dares speak a word against the glorious image that the wisdom of this world has set up. This is the great antichrist, which is nothing but the spirit of Satan working against Christ in the strength and craftiness of earthly wisdom.

Therefore, nothing but a full departure from the wisdom of this world can truly reform the church, and nothing but the nature, Spirit, and works of Christ living in you can be your entrance into the church of salvation. For the church of Christ, as the door of salvation, is nothing else but Christ Himself. Having Christ in us is the same thing as our being in His church. When all that is alive in Christ is also alive and working in you, then you are in His church, for those who are His must be like Him.

Without this, it does not matter what circumstances define your life; it does not matter how educated you are. To everyone except the new creature, Christ says, *"I know you not"* (Matt. 25:12), and to every virtue that worldly wisdom pretends to have, He says, *"Get thee behind me, Satan...for thou savourest not the things that be of God"* (Matt. 16:23). The reason why it must be this way—why worldly wisdom, though it may have a religious form, can only be called Satan or the Antichrist—is that everything we are and have from this world is enmity against God (James 4:4). Everything about us, everything we possess, is the evil that separates us from Him and constitutes all the death and damnation that belongs to our fallen state. Our separation from God is so certain that a total departure from every aspect of worldly wisdom is absolutely necessary to change an evil son of Adam into a holy son of God.

The Whole Purpose of the Church

Here I want you to remember that the church of Christ has this purpose alone: to make us holy as He is holy (1 Pet. 1:16). But nothing can do this except that which has full power to change a sinner into a saint. Anyone who has not found that power in the church may be assured that he is not yet a true son of Christ's church. For Christ's church alone brings forth holy children of God; it has no other purpose, no other nature or work, but that of changing a sinner into a saint.

But this can only be done by something as contrary to the whole nature of sin as light is to darkness. Only something with as much power over it as the light has over darkness can do this. Creeds, canons, articles of religion, stately churches, learned priests, singing, preaching, and praying in the best contrived form of words, cannot raise a dead sinner into a living saint any more than a fine system of light and colors can change the night into day. Indeed, anything that cannot help you to all goodness will not help you to any goodness, and nothing can take away any sin but that which can take away all sin.

On this ground, it is as the apostle said: *"Circumcision is nothing, and uncircumcision is nothing"* (1 Cor. 7:19). On the same ground, it must be said that Catholicism is nothing, and Protestantism is nothing, because, in regard to salvation, everything but a sinner changed into a new creature is nothing. Therefore, only that which takes away all your sins can be called your salvation.

True Membership in Christ's Church

Educated people within the church have given us what they call the marks of the true church. However, whether a person is educated or uneducated, the only proof that he can have as to his own membership in Christ's church is his being dead to all sin and alive to all righteousness. This cannot be more plainly stated than in these words of our Lord: *"Whosoever committeth sin is the servant of sin"* (John 8:34). Surely the servant of sin cannot at the same time be a living member of Christ's body, a new creature who dwells in Christ and has Christ dwelling in him! It is absurd to suppose that a man born again from above is still under a necessity of continuing to sin. Christ has said, *"If the Son therefore shall make you free, ye shall be free indeed"* (v. 36). Truly, if Christ has come to live in you, then a true freedom from all sin has been given to you.

Now, if this freedom from sin is hindered and cannot come to pass in the faithful follower of Christ, can it be because both the willing and working of Christ in man is too weak to overcome that which the Devil wills and works in him? Certainly not! Yet, this absurdity—and even blasphemy—is implied in the very common doctrine that teaches that the Christian can never be done with sinning as long as he lives. If Christians continue to believe this absurdity, they will also continue to live sinfully, without caring whether or not they are doing God's will on earth as it is done in heaven. They will have no concern about being pure, as Jesus who called them is pure, nor will they care to walk as He walked.

The only Christian known to Scripture is the person whose every action is that of a saint. If the saint of Scripture were not a man who shunned all evil and was holy in all his behavior, there would be no real difference between the saint and the carnal man. Preachers and writers comfort halfhearted Christians by telling them that God does not require a perfect, sinless obedience, but that He accepts the sincerity of our weak endeavors instead. Here, if ever, the blind lead the blind.

Paul, comparing the way of salvation to a race, said, *"Know ye not that they which run in a race run all, but one receiveth the prize?"* (1 Cor. 9:24). Now, if Paul could see into the truth of the matter, then they must be blind who teach that God accepts everyone who runs in the religious race and that He does not require that anyone obtain the prize. Paul saw that the sincerity of our weak endeavors is, indeed, quite different from the required perfection of our lives. God accepts our weak attempts at perfection; that is, He bears with them. But He does not do so because He seeks or requires no more. Rather, He bears with them because through them we are moving toward the perfection that He absolutely requires. This perfection is the fullness of the stature of Christ in us, and it is what Paul said is the new creature who obtains the prize.

Paul was saying something that Christ had said in different words: *"Strive to enter in at the strait gate"* (Luke 13:24). In this verse, our best endeavors are called for and are therefore accepted by God. Yet, Christ added, *"For many...will seek to enter in, and shall not be able"* (v. 24). Why is this? It is because

Christ Himself is the one Door into life. Christ said that people strive, and Paul called them runners in a race. Christ called Himself the one Door of entrance, and Paul said that only one receives the prize. That one, who alone obtains the prize or who alone enters through the right door, is that new creature in whom Christ is truly born. Only Christ in us can be our hope of glory.

Is Sin Inevitable?

Those who claim that imperfection is inevitable in this life support their argument by saying that no man in the world, except Christ, was ever without sin. I completely agree with this, and with the apostle I also add, *"If we say that we have not sinned, we make him a liar"* (1 John 1:10). However, if we deny the possibility of our ever being completely freed from sin, then we make Him a liar in that sense, too, for the same Word of God says, *"If we confess our sins, he is faithful and just to forgive us our sins, and to cleanse us from all unrighteousness"* (v. 9).

Surely, if a man is left under a necessity of sinning as long as he lives, he cannot be said to be cleansed from all unrighteousness. How can any logical mind infer that because Christ was the only man who was born and lived free from sin, therefore no man on earth can be raised to a similar freedom from sinning? This is no better than concluding that, because everyone's old nature is descended from Adam, there can therefore be no such thing as a new man created unto righteousness through Christ Jesus living and being all in all in him. Is there any logic in saying that because our Redeemer found us when we were only sinners, He must therefore leave us as sinners?

Christ Himself is the True Vine; therefore, every branch that is His and grows in Him must also have the life and Spirit of the True Vine. As is the vine, so are its branches. If the branch does not have the life and goodness of the vine in it, it must have been broken off from the vine. It is therefore a withered branch, fit only for the fire. But if the branch abides in the vine, then Christ says this about it: *"Ye shall ask what ye will, and it shall be done unto you"* (John 15:7). Now, does this new creature—who is in such union, communion, and power with God because Christ is in him and he is in Christ, as truly as the vine is in the branches and the branches are in the vine—have no choice but to be a servant of sin as long as he lives in this world? If you believe this, then your absurdity is as great as if you had said that Christ must partake of our corruption because He lives within us.

Some people, who abhor the pride of fanatics for the sake of humility, say of themselves and all men, "We are poor, blind, imperfect creatures; all our natural faculties are perverted, corrupted, and out of their right state. Therefore, nothing that is perfect can come from us or be done by us." This is very true, for the apostle said, *"The natural man receiveth not the things of the Spirit of God: for they are foolishness unto him"* (1 Cor. 2:14). This is the man that we all are by nature.

However, is there any Scripture that ever spoke of or required any perfect works from the natural man? Should we think that people are knowledgeable in the things of God if they consider the old natural man to be the Christian, thereby rejecting Christian perfection because this old man cannot attain it? What greater blindness can there be? We cannot rightly appeal to our fallen state as proof of a weakness and corruption that we must have, especially after we have been redeemed from it! This is no better than saying that sin and corruption must be where Christ is because it is where He is not. There is no logic to it at all!

Our Lord truthfully said that unless we are born again from above, there is no possible entrance for us into the kingdom of God (John 3:3, 5). The nature of this new birth in us, and what we get from it, was clearly outlined to us by Christ's beloved apostle, who said, *"Whosoever is born of God sinneth not"* (1 John 5:18). This is as true and unalterable as saying, "That which is born of the Devil can do nothing else but *'add sin to sin'* (Isa. 30:1)."

For what purpose do we daily pray that we will not fall into sin, if it is not possible for us to live even a single day without sin? But if sin can cease in us for one day, can it not do the same for two days? What benefit is there in praying that God's will may be done on earth as it is in heaven, if all men, as long as they are on the earth, must be sinners? Is it not foolish for the church to pray that a baptized person may have power and strength to have victory, and to triumph against the Devil, the world, and the flesh, if this victorious triumph can never be obtained?

It is only foolish if, despite this baptism and prayer, the baptized person must continue committing sin, and so be a servant of sin as long as he lives.

What sense can there be in believing in a communion of saints, if at that same time we are to believe that Christians, as long as they live, must be sinners who follow the lust of the flesh, the lust of the eyes, and the pride of life?

How Long Imperfection Will Prevail

Now, why have these foolish doctrines come about? It is because the church is no longer the spiritual house of God in which only spiritual power and spiritual life are sought after. Rather, it has become a man-made building, consisting of worldly power, worldly learning, and worldly prosperity in gospel matters. Therefore, all the imperfections of human nature now have as much life in the church as in any other human society. Even the best individuals of such a church must be forced to admit that the imperfections of fallen human nature are still alive in all its members, including themselves. Also, imperfection is obviously alive where the continual leading of the Spirit of God is rejected as extreme fanaticism.

Nothing but the full birth and continual breathing and inspiration of the Holy Spirit in the newly born creature can deliver us from all that is earthly, sensual, and devilish in our fallen nature. This new creature, born again in Christ by the eternal Word who created all things in heaven and on earth, is the rock and the church of which Christ said, *"The gates of hell shall not prevail against it"* (Matt. 16:18). Indeed, hell will not prevail against the new creature, though it will prevail against everything else. And every fallen man, no matter who or where he is, is still in his fallen state, and his whole life is in bondage, until the new birth from above has taken him out of it.

The True Church of Salvation

Paul described the church of salvation as being the mother of this new birth. He wrote,

> *Know ye not, that so many of us as were baptized into Jesus Christ were baptized into his death? Therefore we are buried with him by baptism into death: that like as Christ was raised up from the dead by the glory of the Father, even so we also should walk in newness of life.*   *(Rom. 6:3–4)*

Here we have the one true church, infallibly described, and this church is nothing else but the new creature.

Paul continued, *"For if we have been planted together in the likeness of his death, we shall be also in the likeness of his resurrection"* (v. 5). Therefore, to be in Christ or in His church is possible for no one unless the old man is put off and the new creature, risen in Christ, is put on. The same thing is said again in these words: *"Knowing this, that our old man is crucified with him, that the body of sin might be destroyed, that henceforth we should not serve sin"* (v. 6). Consequently, the true church is nowhere but in the new creature, who *"henceforth"* does not sin anymore and is no longer a servant to sin.

All the tedious volumes written about church unity, church power, and church salvation are consequently useless to us. No Council of Trent or assembly of theologians and scholars has a definition of the church. The apostle gave us, not a definition, but the unchangeable nature of it in these words: *"But now being made free from sin, and become servants to God, ye have your fruit unto holiness, and the end everlasting life"* (Rom. 6:22). Having membership in the true church is exactly the same thing as being that new creature in Christ who does not sin.

But what has become of this true church, or where should one go who wants to be a living member of it? He does not need to go anywhere, because wherever he is, the thing that is to save him, and that which he is to be saved from, is always with him. Self is all the evil that he has, and God is all the goodness that he ever can have; but self is always with him, and God is always with him. Death to self is his only entrance into the church of life, and nothing but God can give death to self. Self is an inward life, and God is an inward Spirit of life; therefore, only the inward work of God in the soul, and the inward work of the soul in God, can kill what must be killed in us or bring life to what must come to life in us.

This is the very same religion that the wisdom of this world makes out to be madness! Though it has the same Spirit, the same truth, and the same life that it always had, and though it is the religion of all God's holy angels and saints in heaven, it is considered fanaticism by this world! This is as illogical as saying that temporal things can give life to eternal things! Imagine a Jewish surgeon who laughs at the inward circumcision of the heart, which can only be done by the two-edged sword of God. His idea that such inward circumcision is madness is the same as today's orthodoxy condemning the inward working of God in the soul.

Everything that we can see in this world has no more of salvation in it than the stars and the planets have. All the good works that we can think of have no goodness for us unless the Spirit of God does them in us. This is because the natural man can only go so high. He may do all the outward works of religion; he may observe all church duties and stick close to doctrines; he may put on the semblance of every outward virtue; however, until he is led and governed by the Spirit of God, he can go no higher than this feigned outward formality.

The natural man can use only his own fleshly zeal in defense of such outward attempts at holiness. For all zeal is of the flesh until it is the zeal that is born of God and that calls every creature to the new birth from above. *"My little children,"* said Paul, *"of whom I travail in birth again until Christ be formed in you"* (Gal. 4:19). This is the whole work of an apostle until the end of the world. God's workers have nothing to preach to sinners besides the absolute necessity, the true way, and the certain means of being born again from above.

Why Christ Came

The eternal Son of God came into the world only for the sake of this new birth, to give God the glory of restoring it to all the dead sons of fallen Adam. All the mysteries of this incarnate, suffering, dying Son of God; all the price that He paid for our redemption; all the washings that we have from His all-cleansing blood poured out for us; all the life that we receive from eating His flesh and drinking His blood, have their infinite value, their high glory, and their amazing greatness in the fact that Christ came. Nothing less than these supernatural mysteries of the God-man could raise a new creature out of Adam's death, which could be again a living temple and a habitation of the Spirit of God.

This new birth of the Spirit, or the divine life in man, is the truth, the substance, and the sole purpose of Christ's miraculous mysteries. This was plainly told to us by Christ Himself, who at the end of His ministry on earth told His disciples what was to be the blessed and full effect of it. He pointed to the Holy Spirit, the Comforter (who was now fully purchased for them), who would come after His ascension as a glorious substitute for Christ in the flesh. *"If I go not away,"* said Christ, *"the Comforter will not come unto you; but if I depart, I will send him unto you"* (John 16:7). *"He will guide you into all truth"* (v. 13).

Therefore, all that Christ was, did, and suffered by dying in the flesh and ascending into heaven, was for this sole purpose: to purchase a new birth, new life, and new light for all His followers. The Spirit of God would be restored to them, and would live in them as their supporter, comforter, and guide into all truth. And these were Christ's last words: *"Lo, I am with you alway, even unto the end of the world"* (Matt. 28:20).

Chapter 11

The Spirit of God and the Spirit of This World

In addition to what I have written so far concerning the first state of man and his fall, I must say that the sin of all sins, or the heresy of all heresies, is a worldly spirit. We are apt to consider this characteristic only as a weakness, or a pardonable failure, in ourselves. However, it is indeed the great apostasy from God and the divine life. A worldly spirit is not a single sin, but it is the whole nature of all sin, and there is no possibility that we will come out of our fallen states until it is totally renounced with all the strength of our hearts.

Every other sin, no matter what it may be, is only a branch of the worldly spirit that lives in us. *"There is none good but one,"* said our Lord, *"that is, God"* (Matt. 19:17). In the same way, there is only one life that is good, and that is the life of God and heaven. Depart in the least degree from the goodness of God, and you depart into evil, because nothing is good but His goodness. Choose any life but the life of God and heaven, and you choose death, for death is nothing else but the loss of the life of God.

The creatures of this world have only one life, and that is the life of this world. This is their one life and their one good. Eternal beings also have just one life and one good, but that life is the life of God. The spirit of man is in itself nothing but a spirit breathed forth from the life of God, for the sole purpose that the life of God, the nature of God, the working of God, and the qualities of God might be manifested in the soul.

All the religion of fallen man, all the methods of our redemption, have only one purpose, and that is to take from us that strange and earthly life we have gotten by the Fall, and to kindle again the life of God and heaven in our souls. This is because *"all that is in the world, the lust of the flesh, and the lust of the eyes, and the pride of life, is not of the Father,"* that is, is not the life or the spirit of life that we had from God by our creation, *"but is of the world"* (1 John 2:16). All these worldly things were brought into us by our fall from God into the life of this world.

Therefore, a worldly spirit is not to be considered as a single sin, or as something that may have any degree of Christian goodness. Rather, it ought to be seen as a state of death to the kingdom and life of God in our souls. The heresy of all heresies is a worldly spirit. It is the whole nature and misery of our fall from God; it maintains the death of our souls and, as long as it lasts, makes it impossible for us to be born again from above. It is the greatest blindness and darkness of our nature, and it keeps us in the grossest ignorance both of heaven and hell. Though both heaven and hell are within us, we do not feel either of them as long as the spirit of this world reigns within us. Of all things, therefore, we must detest the spirit of this world, or there is no help for us. If we do not reject the spirit of this world, we will live and die as utter strangers to all that is divine and heavenly.

A worldly, earthly spirit can know nothing of God; it can know nothing, feel nothing, taste nothing, delight in nothing except with earthly senses and after an earthly manner, for it is spiritually dead. Only the life that is in us can feel, taste, understand, like, or dislike. The spirit that directs our lives is the spirit that forms our understanding. It is utterly impossible for us to know God and divine truths until our lives are divine, and wholly dead to the life and spirit of this world. Indeed, our knowledge and understanding can be no better or higher than the state of our lives and hearts.

If you were to ask me, "Why is there so much apostasy in these last times, so much degeneracy in the present Christian church?" I would place all the blame on our having a worldly spirit. In one church you may see open wickedness; in another you may find false forms of godliness. In one worship service you may see superficial holiness, political piety, and crafty prudence, while at another you may find prideful godliness, partial zeal, and envious orthodoxy. Almost everywhere, you may see a blindness and hardness of heart, and the church may be buying and selling with the Gospel, just as the ancient Jews bought and sold beasts in their temple. All these are only so many forms of the worldly spirit. This is the great net with which the Devil becomes a fisher of men, and we may be assured that every son of man is in this net until he breaks out of it by the Spirit of Christ.

I use the words *the Spirit of Christ* because
nothing else can deliver man from the traps of Satan. Nothing can leave the world behind, nothing
can possibly overcome it, except singly and solely the
Spirit of Christ. If we trust in religious observances,
in knowledge, or in the efforts of human wisdom,
then we will overcome one worldly thing only by
cleaving to another.

To see the evil effects of a worldly spirit, we
need only to look at the blessed power and effects of
the spirit of prayer, for the worldly spirit goes
downward with the same strength that the spirit of
prayer goes upward. The spirit of prayer is the one
thing that presses forth out of this earthly life; it
stretches with all its desire after the life of God; it
leaves its own spirit, as far as it can, in order to receive a Spirit from above—to be one life, one love,
and one spirit with Christ in God.

True Religion Has God's Spirit

Here we may firmly conclude that, whatever
shape or form religion may have, it cannot be the
true and proper worship of God unless it worships
and gives itself up to the operation of the holy, triune God, acknowledging that He lives and dwells in
the soul. Indeed, religion can have no good in it, can
do no good to man, can remove no evil from him, and
can raise no divine life in him, but insofar as it is
filled with the Spirit of Christ.

This is the inward religion that is true salvation.
Keep close to this idea of religion as an inward, spiritual life in the soul; seek only the comfort of being
inwardly awakened to all that is holy and heavenly

in your heart; and then, the more you have of this inward religion, the more will you have of a real salvation. Salvation is a victory over man's evil nature; the more you resist and renounce your own vain, selfish, and earthly nature, the more you overcome all the natural tendencies of your *"old man"* (Rom. 6:6). The more God enters into, lives, and operates in you, the more He is the light, life, and Spirit of your soul.

In Him you are that new creature who worships Him in spirit and in truth (John 4:23), for divine worship can only be performed when we are like-minded with Christ. Nothing worships God but the Spirit of Christ, His beloved Son, in whom He is well pleased (Matt. 3:17). If you try to turn religion into anything but a strict, unerring conformity to the life and Spirit of Christ, all your burnt offerings and all your sacrifices will not get you any closer to God. You will be like those who praised God with their lips, but their hearts were far from Him. (See Isaiah 29:13–14.) Unless the Spirit of Christ is alive in it, the heart is always far from God. Only those who have the living Spirit of Christ can walk as Christ walked.

Scripture brings us to the conclusion that all religion is just a dead work unless it is the work of the Spirit of God. All sacraments, prayers, singing, preaching, and hearing are only outward ways of being fervent in spirit, and of giving ourselves more and more to the inward working, enlightening, quickening, and sanctifying of the Spirit of God within us. We do all of this so that the curse of the Fall may be taken from us, so that death may be swallowed up in victory (Isa. 25:8), and so that a

true, real, Christlike nature may be formed in us by
the Spirit.

Why is it so absolutely necessary to turn wholly
to the Spirit of God? Because there must be a continual leader, guide, and inspirer of everything that
lives in nature, and this leader can be either the
Spirit of God, the spirit of Satan, or the spirit of this
world. There is no escape from being directed by one
of these three. The moment you cease to be moved,
quickened, and inspired by God, you are unques-
tionably moved and directed by the spirit of Satan,
by the spirit of this world, or by both of them.

The reason for this is that the soul of man consists only of a birth of God or a birth of nature.
Every moment of the life of man's soul must be lived
in union either with the Spirit of God governing nature, or with the spirit of nature fallen from God and
working in itself. As created beings, we are bound to
live under the guidance and inspiration of some
spirit or power that is greater than our own. Everything that is under our power has been given to us
by our leader. We are led and moved by that spirit to
which we give up ourselves, whether we surrender to
the Spirit of God or to the spirit of fallen nature.

Therefore, if we seek to be always under the inspiration and guidance of God's Holy Spirit, and to
have His divine power in all our actions, we are not
proud fanatics. Rather, by renouncing the Devil and
the world, we Christians act in a way that is suitable
to our state. The Devil and the world can never be
renounced by us unless the Spirit of God is living,
breathing, and moving in us. This is clearly because
only the Spirit of heaven is contrary to the spirit of
Satan and the spirit of the world. God's Holy Spirit

is the only thing that can work contrary to the spirit of this world.

This is why our Lord said, *"He that is not with me is against me; and he that gathereth not with me scattereth abroad"* (Matt. 12:30). In other words, Christ was plainly declaring that to be without Him, and not to be led by His Spirit, is to be led by the spirit of Satan and the world. What is hell? It is nature destitute of the light and Spirit of God, filled only with its own darkness; nothing else can make it to be hell. What is heaven? It is nature awakened, enlightened, blessed, and glorified by the light and Spirit of God dwelling in it.

Here you may see, with the utmost clarity, that to look for salvation in anything else but the Spirit of God living and working within us, and the birth of Christ really brought forth in us, is to be as carnally minded as the Jews were when their hearts were wholly set upon a temporal Savior. This is true because the eternal soul is a spirit breathed forth from God Himself, and so it can only be blessed by having the life of God in it. Nothing can bring the life of God into it except the light and Spirit of God. I personally stand upon this ground in the utmost certainty, looking wholly to the Spirit of God for an inward redemption from all the evil that is in my fallen nature.

The Ministering of the Holy Spirit

Let me now point out to you the true nature of gospel Christianity. I call it "gospel Christianity" in order to distinguish it from the original, universal Christianity that began with Adam. That original

Christianity was the religion of the patriarchs, of Moses and the prophets, and of every penitent man in every part of the world who had faith and hope that God would deliver him from the evil of this world.

When the Son of God took on the nature of humanity, when He finished all the wonders of our redemption and sat down at the right hand of God in heaven, a heavenly kingdom was set up on earth, and the Holy Spirit came down from heaven. The Spirit was given to the flock of Christ in a degree of birth and life that never could have been given until Christ, the Redeemer of the human nature, was glorified. However, when the humanity of Christ, our Second Adam, was glorified, then the heavenly life— the comfort, power, and presence of the Holy Spirit—was the gift that He gave to His friends and followers whom He had left upon earth.

The Holy Spirit descended in the shape of cloven tongues of fire (Acts 2:3) on the heads of those who were the first to receive and administer the new powers of the divine life set up among men. This was the initial manifestation of the whole nature and power of gospel Christianity, very different from what Christianity was before. Thus, the apostles were new men, enrolled into a new kingdom come down from heaven, enlightened with new light, and inflamed with new love. They did not preach something that was absent or distant, but they preached Jesus Christ as the wisdom and power of God, felt and found within them. They preached Christ as the power of God, ready to be communicated as a new birth from above, to all who would repent and believe in Him.

This change of nature, life, and spirit is the true Christianity that believers were then called to preach. They preached an immediate, certain deliverance from the power of sin, to be possessed and governed by the gifts and graces of a heavenly life. And the preachers bore witness, not to a thing that they had merely heard of, but to a power of salvation, a renewal of nature, a birth of heaven, and a sanctification of spirit that they themselves had received. Gospel Christianity then stood upon its own true ground; it appeared to be what it was. And what was it? It was an awakened, divine life set up among men; it was its own proof; it appealed to the heart and conscience of man, which were the only things capable of being touched with these offers of a new life.

The Divine Life Set Up among Men

Sinners of all sorts had begun to feel the burden of their evil natures, and so they were in a state of readiness to receive these glad tidings. While the rigid Pharisees, the orthodox priests, and the rational heathens were at enmity with one another and each proud of their own positions, they all agreed in rejecting and abhorring a spiritual Savior who was to save them from their carnal selves and the vanity of their own selfish virtues. Then, after a while, Christianity lost its first glory, and it was no longer seen as the divine life awakened among men. It was no longer its own proof of the power and Spirit of God manifested in it. Heathen learning and temporal powers were seen as the glory and prosperity of the church of Christ down through the ages, even though the book of Revelation describes such a church as a scarlet whore riding upon a beast (Rev. 17:3–5).

Here, therefore, we must correctly distinguish gospel Christianity from all that went before it or has come after it. It is purely and solely a divine life awakened and set up among men as the effect and fruit of Christ's glorification in heaven. Christianity has no other promise from Him but that of His Holy Spirit, to be our light, our guide, our strength, our comfort, and our protection until the end of the world. Therefore, as gospel Christians, we belong to the new covenant of the Holy Spirit, which is the kingdom of God that came down from heaven on the Day of Pentecost. Also, there is no possibility of seeing or entering into this new kingdom except by being born again of the Spirit.

Though the apostles and disciples of Christ had been baptized with water, had followed Christ, had heard His doctrines, and had done wonders in His name, they were still only *close to* the kingdom of God, and they could only preach that it was soon coming. They had only seen and known Christ as a human being; they had followed Him with great zeal, but with little and very low knowledge of Him and His kingdom. Therefore, they were commanded to stand still, and not to act as His ministers in His new glorified state until they had received power from on high.

They received this power when the Holy Spirit came down upon them with His cloven tongues of fire. Then the apostles and disciples became illuminated instruments of God, intended to spread the light of a heavenly kingdom over all the world. From that day, gospel Christianity was truly distinguished from everything that had gone before it. Christianity was indeed the ministration of the Spirit, and its ministers called the world to nothing but gifts and graces of the same Spirit. Preachers declared that men and women ought to look for nothing but spiritual blessings, to trust, hope, and pray for nothing but the power of that Spirit who was to be the one life and ruling Spirit of this newly opened kingdom of God. No one could join Christians or have any part with them unless he died to the wisdom and light of this world so that he might live by the Spirit through faith in Jesus Christ, who had called him to His kingdom and glory.

This Christianity is its own proof. It requires neither miracles nor outward witness; but, like the sun, it is its own discoverer. Anyone who adheres only to the history, facts, doctrines, and institutions of the Gospel, without being born of its Spirit, is no nearer to Christ. He is like the Jew who carnally adhered to the letter of the law. They both stand far away from gospel Christianity and far away from the true infilling of the Spirit of God.

Chapter 12

The Inward and Outward Churches

In its true nature, religion is both external and internal. The inward truth consists of regeneration, or the life, Spirit, and power of Christ, quickened and brought to life in the soul. The outward sign is the lifestyle that bears full witness to this regenerated life of Christ formed or revealed in the soul. The inward truth gives forth outward manifestations of itself, and these manifestations bring forth the true outward church and make it visible and outwardly known.

Thus, everything in the inward life of Christ—when it begins to live, dwell, and work in our inward man—is the inward church, or the kingdom of God set up within us. And everything we say and do among men in a Christlike manner makes us the members of the outward church that Christ set up in this world.

Inwardly, the only things that lived in Christ were the sole will of God, a perpetual regard for God's glory, and one continuous desire for the salvation of all mankind. When this same spirit is in us, then we are inwardly one with Christ and united to

God through Him. Outwardly, Christ exercised every kind of love, kindness, and compassion toward the souls and bodies of men. In the outward aspect of His life, every form of humility and lowliness of state was visible. He had a total disregard for all worldly riches, power, ease, or pleasure. He had a continuous meekness, gentleness, patience, and submission— not only to the will of God, but also to the haughty powers of the world, to the perverseness and contradiction of all the evil and malice of men, and to all the hardships and troubles of human life.

This outward behavior of Christ is separate from and contrary to the spirit, wisdom, and way of this world. It is the outward church, of which He willed all mankind to become visible and living members. Whoever by the Spirit of Christ lives in the outward exercise of these virtues, also lives in the highest perfection of church unity and is the true inward and outward Christian. He is all that he can be, he has all that he can have, he does all that he can do, and he enjoys all that he can enjoy, as a member of Christ's body, the church, in this world.

Christ was God and man, come down from heaven for the sole purpose of fully restoring the union that had been lost between God and man. The unity of the church is simply the unity of men with God through the power and nature of Christ. Therefore, it must be the truth, and the whole truth, that a man has only to conform to the inward nature and the outward form of Christ's life in order to become a true member of the one church of Christ, outside of which there is no salvation and in which there is no condemnation. This church is the one fold under one Shepherd, though the sheep are scattered or feeding in valleys or on mountains ever so distant and separate from one another.

Let me put the matter this way: true church unity comes when we walk as Christ walked. Our Lord Himself said, *"I am not of this world"* (John 8:23), and, *"Ye are not of the world, but I have chosen you out of the world"* (John 15:19). Therefore, when we are contrary to the world, as Christ was, we fully prove that we are His, that we belong to Him, and that we are one with Him. The following verses from John 15 clarify my point. *"Abide in me, and I in you"* (v. 4). *"If ye abide in me...ye shall ask what ye will, and it shall be done to you"* (v. 7). *"If a man abide not in me, he is cast forth as a branch, and is withered"* (v. 6). *"For without me ye can do nothing"* (v. 5).

Therefore, the one true proof that we are living members of Christ's church on earth, is nothing else but our having the inward nature and the outward behavior that Christ manifested to the world. Conversely, if we are only dead branches fit for the fire, the proof will be that we do not have the Spirit and behavior of Christ. *"This is my commandment, that ye love one another, as I have loved you"* (John 15:12). *"By this shall all men know that ye are my disciples"* (John 13:35). The true and sufficient mark of our outward church membership is found only where the outward form of Christ's loving behavior toward all men is seen.

Spiritual Worship

Not only must our outward behavior be governed by the Holy Spirit, but our worship of God in

His church must also be initiated, carried out, and finished by the Holy Spirit. *"No man can say that Jesus is the Lord, but by the Holy Ghost"* (1 Cor. 12:3). If it is certain that no one can acknowledge Christ as his Lord except by the Holy Spirit, then it must be equally certain that no one can serve or worship God through Christ unless he serves and worships by the power of that same Holy Spirit.

"That which is born of the flesh is flesh" (John 3:6); that is, whatever proceeds from or is done by the natural powers of man, from his nature of flesh and blood, is merely human, earthly, and corrupt. Man's natural powers cannot do anything that is heavenly, or perform a service or worship that is divine, any more than our present flesh and blood can enter into the kingdom of heaven. The apostle said, *"Ye are not in the flesh, but in the Spirit, if so be that the Spirit of God dwell in you. Now if any man have not the Spirit of Christ, he is none of his"* (Rom. 8:9). If we are not His, we can perform no divine service to Him.

Worship cannot cease to be carnal, nor can it become divine, unless it is offered by the power and presence of Christ dwelling in our souls and helping us by His Holy Spirit to cry in truth and reality, *"Abba, Father"* (Gal. 4:6).

The New Testament never calls us to offer anything to God as a divine service or worship except what is done in the truth and reality of faith, hope, love, and obedience to God. But, throughout the New Testament, the only faith, hope, or love that are allowed to be true and godly are the faith, hope, and love that proceed from us solely as a result of the Holy Spirit living, dwelling, and working in us.

This spirituality of the Christian religion is the reason why it was first preached to the world under the name of "the kingdom of God." Under this new dispensation, we are freed from veils, shadows, and images of good things absent or to come. God Himself is manifested, ruling in us and over us as the essential Light of our lives, as the indwelling Word of power, and as the life-giving Spirit within us. He forms us by a new birth, so that we may know that we are a chosen generation and a royal priesthood (1 Pet. 2:9), and so that we may offer spiritual sacrifices to God (v. 5) through the new and living way that Christ has consecrated for us (Heb. 10:19–20).

Therefore, if Christ had not set up this truth of spiritual worship, He would have been just another Moses. And though He was a better teacher, He would have been only a schoolmaster to some higher state of religion that was still to be revealed, if indeed man was to be restored to his true state of life, union, and happiness in and with the divine nature. God is a spirit, and our lives are spiritual; therefore, no religious worship can be in its true perfection, or can bring us into the possession of our highest good, until it raises all that is spirit and life in us into union and communion with the Spirit and life in God.

Becoming a Spiritual Worshipper

So, how we are to become worshippers of the Father in spirit and truth? We may do so by turning inward and focusing on what is daily and hourly stirring, living, and working in our hearts.

There is no passage of Scripture that gives us this direction in exactly these words. However, the

Scriptures do say that God *"dwelleth not in temples made with hands"* (Acts 7:48), but in the temple of our hearts. The kingdom of God is also said to be within us, and not to come with outward signs. It is to be like a secret, living seed of the incorruptible Word in us. The Scriptures also tell us that our hearts are the whole of our lives, and that we live, move, and have our being in God (Acts 17:28). So, they directly tell us that we are to turn inward if we desire to turn to and find God.

God's Word also directly tells us that God abides within us in whatever manner we worship Him. He is our God, our life, our rest and happiness, to the degree that our hearts are willing and choosing, hungering and thirsting, to find, feel, and enjoy the life-giving power of His holy presence in our souls.

Worshipping God with the whole heart and soul, in spirit and in truth, consists of many things. We must be inwardly attentive to God, showing the good and the evil, distinguishing the light from the darkness in our own souls. We must listen to the voice of His ever speaking Word, and watch the movement of His ever sanctifying Spirit within us. We must wait in the spirit of prayer, of faith and hope, of love and yieldedness—wait to be inwardly awakened and revived in the image and likeness of the Son.

Real worship is living to God, in and through the power of Christ, as He lived. It is praying with Him, and by His Spirit, the continual prayer that He always had, whether He was speaking to the multitudes, healing their diseases, or was alone in the still of the night. This inward prayer, in which the whole heart loves, worships, and petitions God—not an absent or distant God, but a Trinity of goodness and mercy, of light and love, of glory and majesty, dwelling and working within us, willing and desiring to do everything in the temple of our hearts that is done in God's own temple in heaven—is a prayer that needs outward words only for the sake of others. Of this prayer we may say to God, as Christ said, *"I knew that thou hearest me always: but because of the people which stand by I said it"* (John 11:42).

Perhaps you will think I have gone too far with this and yet have not come close enough to the matter at hand. But I hope that is not the case. I have tried to show that church unity or communion is not a matter that depends on any particular outward thing, but is complete or defective to the extent that we live in unity with or contrariety to the inward nature and outward example of Christ. For the only union that signifies anything to us or to our salvation, is our union with God through Christ. The only thing that unites us to Christ or makes us His, is His Holy Spirit dwelling and working in us and through us, as He did in Christ.

This is the only church unity that concerns the conscience, and when we are in this unity, we are in union with Christ and with everyone who is united to Him. This is true no matter how separated we may be from each other by human barriers.

The Purpose of Church Services

I myself participate in church services, not because of the purity or perfection of what is done or what is to be found there, but because of what is meant and intended by them. They promote the holy, public worship of God; they are designed to edify

Christians; they are of great use to many people; they keep the world from a total forgetfulness of God; they help uneducated people to find a knowledge of God and the Scriptures that they would not find without such services.

Therefore, although these church assemblies have fallen far from their first spiritual state, I still see them as the venerable remains of all that once was, and hopefully will be again, the glory of the church. This is because the church is still the place for the ministration of the Spirit, and not of the dead letter.

I have witnessed two signs that the day is very near when the church will once again worship in the truth of gospel Christianity. These two signs are found in two very different kinds of people. In the one group of people, there has been an extraordinary increase of new opinions, methods, and religious distinctions. Almost every day, we see them running with eagerness from one method to another; they are searching for something, through the help of a new form, that they were not able to find in an old one.

The vanity and emptiness of a thing is only fully discovered and felt when it has run its entire course and has worked itself up to its highest pitch, so that nothing remains untried even though the deceit remains. Likewise, when religious division, strife over opinions, invented forms, and all outward distinctions have gone as far as they can go and have nothing left to try, then their inevitable fall is at hand.

Even if our zeal were simple and upright, still everything must end in the full conviction that vanity and emptiness, heaviness and deceit, will follow us in every course we take until we no longer try to run our own course. We can only find fulfillment in expecting all and receiving all from the invisible God who dwells in our hearts and blesses us with all heavenly gifts (Eph. 1:3). And we can only expect all and receive all from God when His eternal, all-creating Word and life-giving Spirit are brought forth in our souls.

The other sign I mentioned is to be found in a second group of people. These people are very much awakened, and in the midst of the noise and multiplicity of all church strife, they have heard the still and secret voice of the True Shepherd. They are turned inward, wholly attentive to the inward truth, spirit, and life of genuine religion. They seek the spiritual instruction that leads them to Christ; they are no longer looking here and there for Him, but His redeeming Spirit is within them as the only safe guide from inward darkness to inward light. Having turned from outward shadows to the substantial, ever enduring truth, they have found that the everlasting union of their spirits with God is their only good. Indeed, the life and nature of Christ are truly formed and fully revealed in their souls.

As of now, I find that this is the best way to think about the fallen state of the church. For it is fallen as certainly as it is divided.

In order to secure its place in the heavenly Jerusalem, all that needs to be removed from every church is what may be called its own human will, carnal wisdom, and self-seeking spirit. All of this may be given up as each church turns the eyes and hearts of all its members to an inward adoration of and total dependence upon the supernatural, invisible,

omnipresent God of all spirits. Christians everywhere
need to turn to the inward teachings of Christ as the
power, the wisdom, and the light of God, working
within them every blessing and purity that they can
ever receive either on earth or in heaven.

Under this light, I am neither Protestant nor
Catholic. I cannot say that I belong only to one society of Christians, separate and distinct from all others; to do so would be hurtful to me. The defects,
corruptions, and imperfections in all churches do not
hinder my communion with the church in which I
am now a member, nor do they hinder my being in
full union and hearty fellowship with everything
that is Christian, holy, and good in every other
church. I am part of both the inward church and the
outward church.

I know that God and Christ and the angels take
this position in regard to all that is good in men and
in churches. The variety among men and their
churches reminds me of tares growing with the
wheat (Matt. 13:24–30), so I am not afraid to have
this attitude toward them. Indeed, I am happy to live
and die knowing that God's separate people will one
day be united.

Chapter 13

Christian Ministry

When a Christian is awakened by God, there develops in him a sensitivity to and love for the truths of the Gospel. He wants others to feel and love these truths as much as he does. His first duty, however, is to thankfully, joyfully, and calmly adhere to and allow the increase of this newly risen light within his soul. After truly giving his heart over to God, who is the sole Creator of it, he must humbly beg that everything he hopes will be done in others under his influence, may first be truly and fully done in himself.

The one true way to become more and more awakened, to feel more and more of this first conviction and the work of God within you, is to keep close to the presence and power of God. You do not need to use any powers of reason to force yourself into a deeper awareness of them; there is no need to find more arguments to strengthen them in your mind. Rather, in faith and love, you must draw near to God's presence, which has manifested itself within you. Once you have willingly yielded yourself to His all-creating Word and have become solely dependent upon the work of His Spirit, you will receive the Spirit's power to the degree that you trust Him.

It is by faith that we are saved (Eph. 2:8), because God is always ours in the proportion that we are His. The more faith we put in Him, the more of His power and presence are in us. How wrong it is, therefore, when we turn our thoughts from Him or look for any help but His! For if we ask for everything from Him, if we look to Him to supply all our needs, if we knock only at His door of mercy in Christ Jesus, and patiently wait and abide there, God's kingdom will come, and His will must be done in us.

God is always present and always working on behalf of the life of the soul and its deliverance from captivity of the flesh. But this inward work of God, though never ceasing or altering, is always and only hindered by the activity of our own nature and faculties. Some men hinder God's work through their obedience to earthly passions, and others through striving to be good in their own way—by their natural strength and by doing a great number of seemingly holy works. Both sorts of people obstruct the work of God within their souls.

The only way to cooperate with God is by submitting to His work in our souls. For the whole nature of the fallen soul consists in its being fallen from God and fallen into self-government and activity. Therefore, dying to self—to our reason and to our passions and desires—is the first and indispensable step in Christian redemption. This step brings forth a conversion to God by which Christ becomes formed and revealed in us. When we retain something of our own, such as some form of earthly satisfaction or the righteousness of human endeavors, this conversion is hindered from being fruitful and from obtaining all that we need from God.

Therefore, all the progress of your first conviction, which by the grace of God you have had from above, consists in the simplicity of your faith, in adhering to it as the sole work of God in your soul. This work can only go on in God's way and can never cease to go on in you as long as God continues to be who He is, unless it is stopped by your lack of faith in it or your trusting in something else along with it. God may be found as soon as He alone is sought, but to seek God alone is nothing else but giving ourselves wholly to Him. God is not absent from us unless our spirits and our minds are turned from Him and not left wholly to Him.

This spirit of faith, which in all things looks up to God alone, trusts solely in Him, depends absolutely upon Him, expects everything from Him, and does all it does for Him, is the utmost perfection of piety in this life. The worship of God in spirit and truth can go no higher; it is one power, one spirit, one will, and one working with God. And this is the union or oneness with God in which man was created in the beginning, and to which he is again called and will be fully restored by God and man being made one in Christ.

"Stephen [was] *a man full of faith and of the Holy Ghost"* (Acts 6:5). From this verse, we see clearly that faith and the indwelling of the Holy Spirit are always together; the one can never be without the other.

The gospel dispensation was the beginning of a kingdom of God among men, a spiritual theocracy in which God and man, who was fallen from God, were united in Christ. And so, a union of direct operation between God and man was restored. In order to distinguish it from all that had gone before it, this dispensation was called a direct operation of the Spirit of God in man. It was called the ministration of the Spirit, in which nothing human had any place; all things began in and under obedience to the Spirit, and all things were done in the power and strength of faith united with God.

Therefore, to be a faithful minister of this new covenant between God and man is to live by faith alone, to act only and constantly under its power. The person who lives by faith will desire no will, understanding, or ability except what comes from faith and from a full dependence upon God's direct operation in him.

This is what Peter meant when he wrote,

If any man speak, let him speak as the oracles of God; if any man minister, let him do it as of the ability which God giveth: that God in all things may be glorified through Jesus Christ.

(1 Pet. 4:11)

This is a clear declaration that where this is not done, God is not glorified by Christians through Christ Jesus.

Yielded to God

God created men and angels solely for the glory of His love; therefore, angels and men can give no other glory to God but that of yielding themselves up to the work of His creating love. His love must manifest itself in their natural lives, so that the first creating love, which brought them into being, may go

162

on creating and working in them according to its own never ceasing will, to communicate good forever and ever. They may live to the praise and glory of God by dedicating their entire selves to be mere instruments of His power, presence, and goodness. This is all the glory they can return to their Creator, and all the glory for which He created them. We can give glory to God in no other way than by worshipping Him in spirit and in truth. Christ has said, *"The Father seeketh such to worship him"* (John 4:23).

But we cannot worship God in spirit and in truth unless our spirits truly seek and depend upon the life-giving power of His universal Spirit, and adore Him who is the creator, upholder, and doer of all that is good. For all that is good is done according to the will of God, and all that is according to the will of God is done by His own Spirit. This is unchangeable, whether in heaven or on earth.

This is the one purpose of all the dispensations of God, however various, toward fallen man: to bring man into union with God. You may comply with all the outward modes and institutions of religion; you may believe in all the facts, symbols, figures, representations, and doctrines of Scripture. However, if you use them in any other way, or seek to gain some other good from them, than that of being led out of your own self and your own will, so that the will of God and the Spirit of God may do all that you will and do, then you remain in a fallen state. For the restoration of fallen man is simply his restoration to his first state under the will and Spirit of God, in and for which he was created.

Perhaps, dear reader, you may think that I am being too general, and not specific enough for your situation. But my intention has been to lay the groundwork for proper behavior in every circumstance of the outward work of Christian ministry. All things must be set right in yourself first, before you can rightly assist others toward attaining the same state.

The Purpose of Preaching

The Christian minister, in all his sermons and behavior, ought to turn the attention of men to the power of good and the power of evil, both of which are born and living within everyone. In these two things, or in these two states of the heart of every man, lies the full proof of the whole nature of the Fall and man's redemption from it.

If we were not naturally evil because of evil born and living in us, we would not need redemption. If we did not have something divine in us, we could not be redeemed. Inward evil can only be cured or overcome by an inward good. Therefore, our salvation is an inward work, or a struggle of two powers within us. Consequently, all of a minister's outward instruction must call people to know the state of their hearts. He must call them to seek and find and feel their inward life and death, which have their birth and growth and strife against one another in every son of Adam.

This is the one good way in which to preach. It is also the most powerful way, and it penetrates into the hearts of all men, whatever their condition may be. And this is the true purpose of preaching, namely, to give loud notice of the call of God in men's souls, for this call is always within them, though it is often unheard or neglected by them. Preaching is intended to reach and stir up the inward hearing of the heart. It is meant to strike all the outward senses of the soul, so that the soul may be brought from its insensible sleep into an awakened perception of itself. The soul must be forced to know that the evil of death will be its eternal master unless it seeks victory in the name and power and mediation of Christ, the only Prince of Life and the Lord of Glory, who alone has the keys of heaven, of death, and of hell in His hands.

This is the furthest extent to which the work and ministry of man, in the preaching of the Word, may go.

Preachers must also open the minds of their hearers to a right sense and knowledge of the truth and reality of every virtue and every vice. All that is good and evil is only so to them because it lives in their hearts; they may easily be taught that no virtue, whether it is humility or love, has any goodness unless it springs in and from the heart. People may also be taught that any vice, whether it is pride or anger or something else, cannot be renounced unless its power and place in the heart are destroyed. Thus, the insignificance and vanity of outward formality, virtuous behavior, and everything short of a new heart and new spirit in and through the power of Christ, dwelling vitally in them, may be fully shown to be self-delusion and self-destruction.

The Great Work of the Preacher

A preacher or minister of God should also bring men to an entire faith in, and absolute dependence upon, the continual power and operation of the Spirit of God in them. All churches, even down to those groups who acknowledge God but deny Christ, are forced to believe some of this doctrine in obedience to the letter of Scripture.

For many ages, the church has used education in the arts and sciences in order to qualify ministers for the preaching of the Gospel, as if the position were merely a work of man's wisdom. Clergymen, for the most part, come forth in the power of human qualifications, and they are more or less full of themselves, trusting their own abilities in science, literature, languages, and rhetoric.

To this, more than to any other single cause, the great apostasy of all Christendom is to be attributed. This was the door through which the whole spirit of the world entered into possession of the Christian church. Worldly lusts and interests, vanity, pride, envy, contention, bitterness, ambition, and the death of all that is good in the soul, have always had their nourishment, power, and support from a sense of the merit and sufficiency of human accomplishment. Humility, meekness, patience, faith, hope, contempt of the world, and heavenly emotions (the very life of Jesus in the soul) are hardly practiced or desired by great thinkers, critics, linguists, historians, and public speakers within the church.

Now, the goal of the preacher ought to be to bring people to a full dependence upon and faith in the continual operation of the Holy Spirit, who is the only One who can resurrect and preserve the life of God in their hearts. It is not enough for the clergyman to preach upon the subject every now and then. Rather, everything that he teaches should be constantly directed to it, and he should constantly exhort men to be filled with the Holy Spirit, who is the life and truth of goodness. He should turn his hearers from everything that resists and grieves the blessed Spirit of God, who always desires to remove all evil out of our souls and to make us again sanctified partakers of the divine nature.

Only those who are born again of the Spirit are Christians; therefore, nothing should be taught to Christians unless it is a work of the Spirit, and nothing should be sought in preaching or in hearing except by the power of the Spirit. It is due to the lack of this that there is so much preaching and hearing but so little benefit to either the preacher or the hearer.

Today, it seems as if the work of the preacher is, for the most part, to display logic and eloquence upon religious subjects. However, his religious discourses can no more unite him to God than if he were arguing right and wrong in a court of law. And those who listen to him may go away having been helped to be new men in Christ Jesus just as much as if they had heard a case well pleaded in court. Problems arise when people begin to trust in their own powers. Some preachers trust in their ability to persuade powerfully, and many listeners trust in their ability to act according to what they hear.

And so, the natural man goes on preaching, and the natural man goes on hearing of the things of God, in a fruitless course of life. It will be this way as long as either preachers or hearers seek anything else but the direct power and essential presence of the Holy Spirit working in them.

Therefore, the way to be a faithful and fruitful laborer in the vineyard of Christ is to put yourself in full dependence upon the Spirit of God. Consider yourself as having no good power but as His instrument and by His influence, in all that you do. You must call others, not to their own strength or rational powers, but to a full hope and faith of having all that they need from God alone. You should not teach them to be good according to human wisdom, but by outward instruction you should call them to God Himself—to a rebirth of essential, inherent, living goodness, wisdom, and holiness from His own eternal Word and Holy Spirit living and dwelling in them.

God is all that the fallen soul needs, and nothing but God alone can communicate Himself to the soul. Therefore, everything is lost effort unless the soul is completely converted to the direct, essential operation of God and His Spirit in it.

Chapter 14

How to Be
in the Truth

I have heard one minister say that, after twenty years of zeal and labor in matters of religion, his efforts have done little good. I remember him saying that he felt forced to ask, "Where should I go, or what should I do, to be in the truth?"

The good of true religion is in its ability to revive and awaken the divine nature that our first father originally had from God, and nothing can revive it but that which first created it. God is not your God in any respect unless He is the God of your life, and is manifested in it. Also, He cannot be the God of your life unless His Spirit is living within you.

The only way in which Satan can know you or can have any other fellowship with you, is when his evil spirit works and manifests itself along with the workings of your own spirit. James told us, *"Resist the devil, and he will flee from you"* (James 4:7), but the Devil can only be resisted as a spirit working within the heart. Therefore, to resist the Devil is to turn from the evil thoughts and inclinations that arise within your own heart.

169

James went on to write, *"Draw nigh to God, and he will draw nigh to you"* (v. 8). God is a universal Spirit that you cannot physically turn to or from; therefore, to turn to God is to cleave to those good thoughts and inclinations that proceed from His Holy Spirit dwelling and working in you.

This is the God of your life, to whom you are to adhere, listen, and attend; and this is how you may worship Him in spirit and in truth. The Devil goes about *"as a roaring lion"* (1 Pet. 5:8), and he has no voice but that which he speaks within you. Therefore, know and understand all that goes on within your heart, for whether you delight in good or grieve over evil, you could not recognize either unless a holy God of light and love dwelled in you. Do not seek any other road, or call anything the way to God, except that which His eternal, all-creating Word and Spirit work within you. For if anything else could have been man's way to God, the Word would not have come in the flesh.

Putting Aside the Veil

My minister friend wondered how he could be in the truth. Indeed, how does one come to be in the truth? Christ Himself declared, *"Ye shall know the truth, and the truth shall make you free"* (John 8:32)—free from the blindness and delusion of your own natural reason, and free from forms, doctrines, and opinions that others impose upon you.

To be in the truth is the finished state of man returning to God. To be in the truth is to be where the first holy man was when he came forth in the image and likeness of God. When he lost Paradise, he lost the truth; and all that he felt, knew, saw, loved, and liked of the earthly, bestial world into which he had fallen was mere separation from God, a veil upon his heart and scales upon his eyes. The first truth that he had received could not be spoken of to him, even by God Himself, except under the veil of earthly things, types, and shadows. The Law was given by Moses, but Moses had a veil upon his face. The Law was a veil, prophecy was a veil, Christ crucified was a veil, and all was a veil until grace and truth came by Jesus Christ in the power of His Holy Spirit.

Therefore, to be in the truth, as it is in Jesus, is to have come from under the veil, to have passed through all those dispensations that would never have begun if they did not end with Christ spiritually revealed and truly formed in the soul. Now, in this last dispensation of God, which is the first truth itself restored, nothing is to be thought of, trusted in, or sought except God's direct, continual working in the soul by His Holy Spirit. This is where you are to go and what you are to do, to be in the truth.

The truth, as it is in Jesus, is nothing else but Christ come in the Spirit, and His coming in the Spirit is nothing else but the first lost life of God awakened and revealed again in the soul. Everything short of this has only the nature of an outward type, which in its best state lasts only for a time.

Therefore, if you look to anything but the Spirit, seek any power but that of the Spirit, expect Christ to be your Savior in any other way than by His being spiritually born in you, you go back from the grace and truth that came by Jesus, and at best you can be only a legalistic Jew or a self-righteous Pharisee.

You cannot get any further than these states except by being born of the Spirit, by living in the Spirit as His child, His instrument, and His holy temple in which He dwells and works all His good pleasure.

If you leave out this full adherence to and dependence upon the Spirit, if you act as if you can be something through your own wisdom and ability, then—even though your words are the outward words of the spiritual Gospel and your actions are the outward practices of the apostles—you are like one who worshipped God with the blood of bulls and goats. For only the Spirit of God can worship God in spirit and in truth.

The Continual Guidance of the Spirit

But perhaps you will say that you are still in a poor state because you do not know how to find the continual guidance of the Holy Spirit. If you know how to find your own thoughts, you can easily find the Spirit of God, for every thought within you is either from the good of the Spirit or from the evil of the flesh. Now, the good and the evil that are within you can teach you of the work and presence of the Spirit of God. For the good could not appear as good, nor could the evil be felt as evil, unless the direct working of the Spirit of God in you created or manifested this difference between them.

Therefore, whatever state you are in, the power of God's Spirit within you equally manifests itself to you. To find the direct and continual working of the Spirit of God within you, you need only to know and feel the good and evil that are within you. Every good thought or desire in you is only evidence of God within you, and when you follow a good thought, you follow the Spirit of God. On the other hand, every selfish and wicked thought or emotion is evidence of the spirit of Satan within you, which would not be known or felt as evil except that it is contrary to the direct, continual working of the Spirit of God within you.

Look within your own heart, therefore, and all that is within you will demonstrate to you the presence and the power of God in your soul. You will find and feel it with the same certainty as you find and feel your own thoughts. Best of all, by turning inward, you will always have a living sense of the direct guidance and inspiration of the Holy Spirit. His inspiration is always equal to your dependence upon it, always leading you from strength to strength in your inward man, until all your knowledge of good and evil is simply a love of good and an aversion to evil.

Remember, the one work of the Spirit of God is to distinguish the good and evil that are within you. When you are wholly given up to this new-creating work of God, fix your mind upon it, abide with it, and expect everything from it. This, my friend, will enable you to return to the rock from which you were hewn (Isa. 51:1), to drink at the fountain of living waters (Jer. 2:13), to walk with God, to live by faith, to put on Christ, to continually hear the Word of God, to eat the Bread that came down from heaven (John 6:41), to fellowship with Christ, and to follow the Lamb wherever He goes (Rev. 14:4).

All these seemingly different things will be found in every man, according to his measure, who is wholly given up to and dependent upon the blessed work of God's Spirit in his soul.

Redemption of the Soul

The mistake that most Christians make is this: they want to be good by some outward means; to have methods, opinions, forms, and ordinances of religion; to alter and raise their fallen nature and to create a new heart and a new spirit in themselves. In other words, they desire to be good in a way that is altogether impossible, for goodness cannot be brought into anyone through any outward action, much less by anything that is human.

The image and likeness of Father, Son, and Holy Spirit are in every man, going before every outward work or action that can proceed from him. God within him is the sole reason why anything that he does or practices can be called godly. If it were not so, man would have only his being from God, but his goodness from himself.

All man's outward good works are only like the good words that he speaks. He is not a better person because he uses them frequently; they bring no goodness into him, nor are they of any worth in themselves. Their only value lies in the fact that a good and godly spirit goes forth in the sound of them. This is the case with every outward, creaturely thing or work of man, whether it is hearing, praying, singing, preaching, or practicing any outward duties. All these things may have only the goodness of one who follows the law but has no Christ in his heart. These things are as fruitless as *"sounding brass, or a tinkling cymbal"* (1 Cor. 13:1), unless they are solely the work and fruits of the Spirit of God. Indeed, the divine nature is the only thing that can be the power of any good work, either in men or angels.

When a man first finds himself stirred up with religious zeal, what does he generally do? He turns all his thoughts outward, he runs after this or that great speaker, he is at the beck and call of every new opinion, and he thinks only of finding the truth by resting in some new religious method or group of Christians. If he could find a leader who could truly turn him from the teachings of man toward God Himself—not the God historically read about in books or preached about in various circles, but the God truly living and working in every heart—such a leader he might call a man of God.

If a man had a hundred things, but these things were not calls to respond to Christ who has come in the Spirit, to God within him, as the only possible light and teacher of his mind, it would be a hundred times better for him to be without them. For all man's blindness and misery lies in this: he has lost the knowledge of God living within him, and he has fallen under the power of an earthly, bestial life. He thinks of God as living in some other world, and so he seeks to set up an image of an absent God, instead of worshipping the God of life and power in whom he lives, moves, and has his being (Acts 17:28).

Therefore, whoever teaches you to expect great things from a certain set of opinions, or says that something can save or redeem besides the manifestation of God in your own soul through a birth of the holy nature of Christ within you, is totally ignorant of the whole nature of both the Fall and the redemption of man. For the Fall was a death to the divine life or Christlike nature that lived in the first man, and redemption is Christ newly born, formed, and

175

revealed again in man as He was at the first. These two great truths were most strongly asserted by Christ when He said, *"If any man will come after me, let him deny himself, and take up his cross, and follow me"* (Matt. 16:24).

"Let him deny himself" is the fullest proof that man has lost his first divine and heavenly nature, that he is not the original self that came from God. Otherwise, he could not be called to deny it. You may say that man has not lost that first heavenly life in God; in that case, you must say that our Lord calls man to deny, crucify, and renounce the holy and godlike self that was the first gift of God to him. This certainly cannot be the case!

Our Incapacity for Goodness

I have known many people who appear to be in a state of confusion, because their heads and their hearts are so contrary—the one delighting in heavenly things, the other governed by earthly passions and pursuits. The best thing for their situation is that they know and acknowledge their position, for only through this truth, through the full and deep perception of it, can they have any entrance into the liberty of the children of God. In this respect, God is dealing with them as He does with those whose darkness is to be changed into light. But this can never be done until people fully know the real badness of their hearts and their utter inability to deliver themselves from it by any power or activity of their own minds.

Suppose this is your situation, and suppose that you see yourself in a better state than you really are in. Although you are not aware of the badness in your heart, it is still there, and to conceal it would only be to your greater hurt. For whether it is seen and found or not, it is certainly there, and sooner or later it must show itself in its full deformity. Otherwise, the old man will never die the death that is due to him and that must be undergone before the new man in Christ can be formed in us.

Everything that you find to be wrong in your heart is common to natural man; there is no heart that is without it. And this is the one reason why every man, however different he may be in character, appearance, or abilities from others, has the same absolute necessity of being born again from above. The fleshly nature, and the spirit of this world, govern every spring in the heart of the natural man. Therefore, you can never have enough adoration for the ray of divine light that, breaking in upon your darkness, has shown this to be the state of your heart and has raised up faint wishes to be delivered from it.

Even if such desires for deliverance are faint, they have a degree of goodness in them, and they proceed solely from the goodness of God working in your soul. You may, therefore, believe that your awareness of your incapacity for goodness is a heavenly seed of life and the blessed work of God in your soul.

If there were any good in your heart, or if you had any power of your own to embrace and follow the truth, you would be turning away from God and all goodness, and building iron walls of separation between God and your soul. This is because conversion to God only begins to be true and real when we see that nothing in ourselves can give us the least degree of faith, hope, trust, or comfort.

It is one thing to see all outward things as vanity and to hate and abhor certain sins, but it is quite another thing to see the vanity within ourselves and to believe ourselves to be utterly unable to take one single step in true goodness. Under this conviction, the gate of life is open to us. Therefore, all the preparatory parts of religion and all the various proceedings of God over either our inward or outward state—such as setting up and pulling down, giving and taking away, light and darkness, comfort and distress—are all for this one purpose: to cause us to believe that everything that can be called life, goodness, and happiness is to come solely from God, and not the smallest spark of it from ourselves.

When man was first created, all the good that he had was from God alone. Has anything changed since then? No, this is the state of man forever. From the beginning of time through all eternity, man can have no goodness but that which God creates in him.

Our first created goodness was lost because our first father departed from a full, absolute dependence upon God. Only a full, continuous, unwavering dependence upon God can keep God in the creature, and the creature in God. Until the power of Christ lives in us and we are brought out of ourselves and all selfishness, our lost goodness can never come again or be found in us, and we will not move into that full and blessed dependence upon God in which our first father should have lived.

Now, my dear friend, do you have any room to complain about being so aware of your inability to make yourself better than you are? If you lacked this awareness, every part of your religion would have the nature and vanity of idolatry. For you cannot come unto God, you cannot believe in Him, you cannot worship Him in spirit and truth, until He is regarded as the only Giver, and you yourself as nothing else but the receiver, of every heavenly good that can possibly come to life in you.

How can it trouble you that it was God who made you, and not you yourself? How unreasonable! God must forever be God alone; heaven and the heavenly nature are His, and must forever be received only from Him and preserved by an entire dependence upon and trust in Him. All of the genuine religion of fallen man, fallen from God into himself and into the spirit of this world, has no other purpose but to bring us back to an entire dependence upon God. Blessed is the light and the conviction that bring us into a full and settled despair of ever having the least good from ourselves! When we can say this, we are truly brought and laid at the gate of mercy, at which no soul can lie down in vain.

A broken and contrite heart God will not despise (Ps. 51:17). That is, God will not, He cannot, pass by, overlook, or disregard it. But the heart is only broken and contrite when all its strongholds are broken down, when all false coverings are taken off, and when it sees, with inwardly opened eyes, everything that proceeds from within itself and not from God is bad, false, and rotten.

But perhaps you will say that your conviction is only an uneasy awareness of your own state, and it does not have the goodness of a broken and contrite heart. This may be true, but this is how conviction begins. Conviction is not always full and perfect; if it were, would you complain about your inability to help or mend yourself? No, you would patiently expect help from God alone.

Therefore, know that you lack all goodness. But, at the same time, know that goodness cannot be had through your own willing and running, but only through *"God that showeth mercy"* (Rom. 9:16), that is, through God who gives us Jesus Christ. For Jesus Christ is the mercy of God to all the fallen world.

Now, if all the mercy of God is to be found only in Christ Jesus; if He alone can save us from our sins; if He alone has power to heal all our infirmities and to restore original righteousness, we have no room to complain about any of our own attempts. Our only questions should be where and how Christ is to be found.

It does not matter what our evils are—deadness, blindness, intemperance, hardness of heart, covetousness, wrath, pride, or ambition. Our remedy is always one and the same, always at hand, always certain and infallible. Christ can cast out seven devils as easily as He can cast out one. He came into the world, not to save us from one disorder or another, but to destroy all the power and works of the Devil in man.

How You Can Find Christ

So then, where and how is Christ to be found? He is to be found in your heart, and nowhere else; He is to be found by your heart, and by nothing else.

But perhaps you will object that your own heart keeps you a stranger to Christ, and Him to you, because your heart is all bad, as unholy as a den of thieves. However, when you find this to be the state of your heart, you begin to really find Christ in it. For nothing else but Christ can reveal the sin and evil that are in you. And He who makes these things manifest is the same Christ who takes away sin. Therefore, as soon as you feel the guilt of your state, you may be assured that Christ is in you indeed.

For Christ must first come as a discoverer and reprover of sin. It is the infallible proof of His holy presence within you. Hear Him, reverence Him, submit to Him as a discoverer and reprover of sin. Acknowledge His power and presence in the feeling of your guilt, and then He who wounded you will heal you, He who found out the sin will take it away, and He who showed you your den of thieves will turn it into a holy temple of the Father, Son, and Holy Spirit.

You have no freedom to assume any holy disposition, nor can you use any willpower of your own to take hold of the goodness that you would like to have. For nothing can ever be goodness in you but the one life, light, and Spirit of Christ revealed in your soul. Christ in us is our only goodness, just as Christ in us is our *"hope of glory"* (Col. 1:27). Christ in us is the pure, free gift of God to us.

You may not have the freedom to make yourself holy, but you do have a true and full freedom either to give up your helpless self to the operation of God on your soul, or to rely upon your own rationality and natural strength of mind. This is the freedom of your will, and this is a freedom that every man, regenerate or unregenerate, has as long as he is alive on this earth.

Therefore, if you do not have what you want to have from God, or if you are not what you ought to be in Christ Jesus, it is not because you have no power of choice to leave yourself in the hands and under the operation of God. Rather, it is because the same power of choice has caused you to seek help where it cannot be had, namely, in some strength and activity of your own faculties or those of other men.

Concerning this freedom of will, Christ said, *"According to your faith be it unto you"* (Matt. 9:29). In other words, to the degree that you leave yourself in God's hands and trust yourself to Him, He will operate in you. This is the real power of turning the will toward God.

When this freedom of the will wholly leaves itself to God, saying, *"Not my will, but thine, be done"* (Luke 22:42), then it has all that it desires. The will of God is done in it; it is in God; it has divine power; it works with God and because of God. The soul comes at last to the kind of faith that can move mountains, and nothing is too hard for it.

And so, every unregenerate son of Adam has life and death in the power of his own choice. With full freedom, he may choose either to entrust himself to the redeeming operation of God, which is eternal life, or to act according to his own will and power in the flesh, which is eternal death. Here lies all true freedom, which cannot be taken from you. Your road to heaven lies in the constant exercise of this freedom, that is, in continually depending upon the operation of God in your soul. No divine virtue can be had any other way.

The true graces of the spiritual life, including faith, hope, love, and patience, have their source in this free and complete surrender of oneself to God. They are only expressions of your willing nothing, seeking nothing, and trusting nothing but the life-giving power of His holy presence in your soul.

In summary, you must wait patiently, trusting humbly and depending only upon the God of light and love, mercy and goodness, glory and majesty. Seek Him and Him alone, and He will always dwell in the inmost depth and spirit of your being. The blessed operations of the Upholder of all creation will always be found by a humble, faithful, loving, calm, patient introversion of your heart to Him. He has His hidden heaven within you, and it will open itself to you as soon as you leave your heart completely to His eternal, ever speaking Word and His ever sanctifying Spirit within you.

Nevertheless, beware of all eagerness and activity of your own natural spirit and temperament. Do not be in a hurry to follow any of your own ways. Be patient under the sense of your own vanity and weakness; patiently wait for God to do His own work, in His own way. Remember, you cannot go any faster than a full dependence upon God can carry you.

Perhaps you will say, "Am I to be idle, then, and to do nothing toward the salvation of my soul?" No, you must by no means be idle, but be earnestly diligent, according to your ability, in all good works that the Law and the Gospel direct you to. Other people may justly consider your outward good works as God's errand on which you are sent. Therefore, they are to be done faithfully, according to His will and in obedience to Him who sent you.

Even so, nothing that you do or practice as a good to yourself or other people, is in its proper state, grows from the right root, or reaches its true end until you depend upon doing good only through Christ, the wisdom and power of God living in you. Be careful of the eagerness and activity of your own nature, for they may lead you to seek and trust in something that is not God or Christ within you.

Faith needs its proper soil in which to grow. Therefore, I recommend that you be still and patient, so that you do not become lifeless or indifferent about good works. When we are eager and restless, when we are impatient either with regard to God or ourselves, these are not only great hindrances, but also real defects of our faith and dependence upon God.

Lastly, be courageous and full of hope, not by looking at any strength of your own or by imagining that you now know how to be wiser than you have been so far. This will only help you to find more and more defects and weaknesses in yourself. Instead, be courageous in faith and hope and dependence upon God, and be assured that the one infallible way to reach all that is good is never to be weary in waiting, trusting, and depending upon God manifested in Christ Jesus.

Chapter 15

Returning to God

E very evil, whether inward or outward, should only teach you one truth: man has unmistakably lost his first divine life in God, and no possible comfort or deliverance is to be expected except through Christ. Though man lost God, God became man so that man might again be alive in God, as he was in the beginning. All the misery and distress of human nature, whether of body or mind, comes about solely because God is not in man, nor man in God, as the condition of his nature requires. Man has lost the first life of God in his soul—the life in and for which he was created. He lost this light and spirit and life of God by turning his will, thoughts, and desires into a taste for the good and evil of this bestial world.

Now, there are two things that have taken the place of the life of God in man. First, self, or selfishness, was brought forth by man's choosing to have a wisdom of his own, contrary to the will and instruction of his Creator. Secondly, an earthly, bestial, mortal life and body were brought forth when man ate the food that poisoned his paradisiacal nature. Both of these must therefore be removed; that is, a man must first totally die to self, to all earthly desires, views, and intentions, before he can again be in God as his nature and first creation requires.

But now, it is absolutely and immutably true that man, as long as he is a selfish, earthly-minded creature, must be deprived of his true life—the life of God, the spirit of heaven, in his soul. In light of this truth, everything is changed! For then, there is no life that ought to be as dreaded as a life of worldly ease and prosperity. There is great misery, a great curse, in everything that gratifies and nourishes our self-love, self-esteem, and self-seeking! On the other hand, there is great happiness in all spiritual and physical troubles when they force us to feel and to know the hell that is hidden within us and the vanity of everything around us. Our troubles turn all our self-love into self-abhorrence, and they force us to call upon God to save us from ourselves, to give us a new life, new light, and a new spirit in Christ Jesus.

The Spirit of Prayer

Your present and past distresses should bring you to acknowledge this twofold truth that I have stressed over and over again: first, you are nothing but darkness, vanity, and misery in and of yourself; secondly, you cannot help yourself to light and comfort by any effort of your own. I know that many people seem to assent to these two truths, but their belief has no depth or reality, and so it is of little or no use. However, some people, and perhaps you, have opened their hearts to a deep and full conviction of these truths. If you believe these two truths

with as much certainty as you know that two plus
two equals four, then you, like the Prodigal Son,
have come to your senses, and more than half your
work is done.

Now, if you fully possess these two truths, you
will feel them in the same degree of certainty as you
feel your own existence. Under this awareness, you
are to give up yourself absolutely and entirely to God
in Christ Jesus, as if you were falling into the hands
of infinite love. It is a great and infallible truth that
God's will for you consists only of infinite love and
an infinite desire to make you a partaker of His divine nature. It is absolutely impossible for the Father of our Lord Jesus Christ to refuse to give you all
the good and life and salvation that you need.

Drink deeply from this cup, for the precious water of eternal life is in it! Turn to God with this
faith; cast yourself into this abyss of love; and then
you will be in the state that the Prodigal Son was in
when he said, *"I will arise and go to my father, and
will say unto him, Father, I have sinned against
heaven, and before thee, and am no more worthy to
be called thy son"* (Luke 15:18). And everything will
be fulfilled in you that is recorded of the Prodigal
Son.

Therefore, make this the twofold practice of
your heart: first, bow yourself down before God in
the deepest acknowledgment of your own nothing-
ness and vileness; then, look up to God in faith and
love, and consider Him as always extending the arms
of His mercy toward you. God is full of an infinite
desire to dwell in you as He dwells in the angels in
heaven. Content yourself with this inward and simple exercise of your heart for a while, and seek the

things that nourish and strengthen this state of your heart.

"Come unto me," said Jesus, *"all ye that labour and are heavy laden, and I will give you rest"* (Matt. 11:28). This is more for you to rest upon—more light for your mind and more blessing for your heart than all the volumes of human instruction can provide. Take hold of the words of Jesus, and beg Him to be the light and life of your soul. Love the sound of His name, for Jesus is the love, the sweetness, and the compassionate goodness of the Deity, who became man so that men might have *"power to become the sons of God"* (John 1:12). Love every soul in the world; dwell in love, and then you will dwell in God; hate nothing but the evil that stirs in your own heart.

Teach your heart the following prayer, until you continually say it: "Holy Jesus, meek Lamb of God, Bread that came down from heaven, Light and Life of all holy souls, help me to have a true and living faith in You. Open Yourself within me, with Your holy nature, Spirit, and inclinations, so that I may be born again in You. Make me a new creature, revived, led, and governed by Your Holy Spirit." When you practice this prayer, it will become the life of your soul and the true food of eternity. Remain in this state of supplication to God, and then you will infallibly be raised out of the vanity of time into the riches of eternity.

Do not expect to have the same degree of fervor each and every time you pray. This is not where the heart of the matter lies. Your human body will have its share in the praying, but the ups and downs of that are to be overlooked. When your will is set in the right place, the changes of human fervor do not lessen your union with God.

The heart, which is an unfathomable depth of eternity within us, is as much above outward fervor as heaven is above earth. It is the heart that works our way to God and unites us with heaven. This depth of the heart is the divine nature and power within us, which never calls upon God in vain. Whether assisted or deserted by outward fervor, the heart penetrates through the outward nature as easily and effectively as our thoughts can leave our bodies and reach into the regions of eternity.

The poverty of our fallen nature, the depraved workings of the flesh, the corrupt tendencies of our polluted birth into this world, do us no harm as long as the spirit of prayer works contrary to them and longs for the first birth of the light and Spirit of heaven. All our natural evil ceases to be our own evil as soon as our wills turn from it. Then it changes its nature, loses all its poison and death, and only becomes our holy cross on which we happily die to self and this world and enter the kingdom of heaven.

Do you want to be free of error, reservations, and delusion about where you stand with God? Consider the Deity to be the greatest love, the greatest meekness, the greatest sweetness. Consider His eternal, unchangeable will to be a blessing to every creature. Then recognize that all the misery, darkness, and death of fallen angels and fallen men came about because they lost their likeness to this divine nature. You and the entire fallen world have nothing to wish for except that rays and sparks of this divine, meek, loving, tender nature of God will be drawn into the life of your soul by the spirit of prayer.

Consider Jesus as the gift of God to your soul, which begins and completes the birth of God and heaven within you, in spite of every spiritual or physical enemy. When you have heartily embraced these infallible truths and made them the nourishment of your soul, your way to heaven will be shortened and secured, and there will be no room for error, reservations, or delusion.

You can expect no life, light, strength, or comfort except from the Spirit of God dwelling and manifesting His own goodness in your soul. The best men and the best books can only do you good insofar as they turn you to seek and receive every kind of good from God alone—not a distant or an absent God, but a God living, moving, and always working in the spirit and heart of your being.

Those who seek God with their minds and their ideas will never find God, because God is the highest Spirit and the highest life, and only a similar spirit and life can unite with Him or know anything about Him. Therefore, faith, hope, and love, when they are turned toward God, are the only possible and infallible means of obtaining a true and living knowledge of Him. The reason for this is clear: through the spiritual workings of life within us, we seek the God of life where He is; we call upon Him with His own voice; we draw near to Him by His own Spirit. For no physical body, no flesh and blood, can breathe forth faith and love and hope to God without having the Spirit and life that is of God.

The most infallible truth in the world is that neither reasoning nor learning can ever introduce a spark of heaven into our souls. Therefore, you have nothing to seek, and nothing to fear, from reason.

Life and death are the things in question; although neither contributes to the growth of reasoning or learning, each is a state of the soul. Their only difference is that life is the enjoyment of the soul's highest good, and death is the lack thereof.

Therefore, reason and learning have no power here. Their attempts to keep the soul insensitive to life and death—one of which is always developing in the soul according to the will and the desires of the heart—are in vain. If you were to add intelligence to a vegetable, you would be adding nothing to its life or death. Its life and fruitfulness lie only in the soundness of its root, the goodness of the soil, and the riches it derives from air and light. It is the same for man.

This is how heaven and hell grow in the soul of every man. His heart is the root, and if the heart is turned away from all evil, it is then like a plant in good soil. When it hungers and thirsts after the divine life, it then infallibly draws the light and Spirit of God into it, which are infinitely ready and willing to live and bear fruit in the soul. For the soul has its breath, its being, and its life for no other purpose than that the triune God may manifest the riches and powers of His own life in it.

Giving Up All for God

Everything that lives partakes of life, every being hungers after the source of its existence, and every creature can only find its rest in the place from which it came. Dead as well as living things bear witness to this truth: the stones fall to the earth and *"the sparks fly upward"* (Job 5:7) only because

191

everything must go back to the place from which it came. If the souls of men were not breathed forth from God as real offspring of the divine nature, it would be as impossible for them to have any desire for God as for stones to go upward and the flame to go downward. The spirit of prayer is the one thing that proves that you came from God, and it is your certain way of returning to Him.

Therefore, when it is the never ceasing desire of our hearts that God may be the beginning and end, the reason and motive, the rule and measure, of all that we do, then we are offered up to the eternal Spirit of God. Our lives will be in Him and from Him, and we will be united to Him by the spirit of prayer that is the comfort, support, strength, and security of the soul. By the help of God, we will travel through the vanity of time into the riches of eternity.

In order to have this spirit of prayer, let us willingly give up all that we inherit from our fallen father, so that we may hunger and thirst after God alone. Our only care ought to be how we can be wholly His devoted instruments, His adoring, joyful, and thankful servants in everything. We must be sure to shut our eyes and cover our ears to everything that is not a step in the ladder that reaches from earth to heaven.

Reading, listening, talking, and meditating are all good things, but they are only good at certain times and to a certain degree. They must be used with much caution, or they will bring forth in us the fruits of intemperance. But the spirit of prayer is for all times and all occasions; it is a lamp that is to be always burning, a light to be ever shining. Everything calls for it, and everything is to be done in it and governed by it. Indeed, the spirit of prayer is nothing else but the spirit of a man wholly and incessantly given up to God, to be all that He pleases.

This state of absolute yieldedness, naked faith, and pure love of God is the highest life of those who are born again from above and have become sons of God through the divine power. It is exactly what our blessed Redeemer called us to aspire to when He spoke these words: *"Thy kingdom come. Thy will be done in earth, as it is in heaven"* (Matt. 6:10). It is to be sought with the simplicity of a little child, without being captivated by any mysterious speculations. Everything about it should bring us nearer to God; should force us to forget and renounce everything for Him; should cause us to do everything in Him, with Him, and for Him; and should spur us to give every breath, movement, intention, and desire of our hearts, souls, spirits, and lives to Him.

Notice what our blessed Lord said of the place, the power, and the origin of truth. He did not refer us to the current doctrines of the times, or to the systems of men, but to His own name, His own nature, and His own divinity hidden in us. *"My sheep,"* He said, *"hear my voice"* (John 10:27). Here, the whole matter is decisively determined, both where truth is and who can have any knowledge of it.

Heavenly truth is spoken only by the voice of Christ, and it is only heard by the power of Christ living in the hearer. He is the eternal Word of God, who speaks forth all the wisdom and wonders of God. He alone is the Word, who speaks forth all the life, wisdom, and goodness that can be in any creature. The soul can have no goodness or wisdom or life except what it has in Him and from Him. This is the one unchangeable boundary of truth, goodness, and every perfection of men on earth or angels in heaven.

Literary learning, from the beginning to the end of time, will always have very little of heavenly wisdom and very much of worldly foolishness. Its nature is one and the same through all ages; what it was in the Jew and the heathen, it is in the Christian, too. Its name and its nature are unalterable, for it is always foolishness in the eyes of God.

Recommendations to the Christian

Allow me to take a few more pages in this chapter in order to recommend the following actions to you.

First, willingly receive every spiritual and physical trouble, every disappointment, pain, uneasiness, temptation, darkness, and desolation. These are true opportunities and blessed occasions for dying to yourself and entering into a fuller fellowship with your self-denying, suffering Savior. Do not look at spiritual or physical trouble in any other light; reject every other thought about it. Then, every kind of trial and distress will become the blessed day of your prosperity.

Secondly, be afraid of seeking or finding comfort in anything but God alone, for anything else that gives you comfort will take your heart away from God just a little bit more. What constitutes a pure heart? In a pure heart, God alone is totally and purely sufficient, and God alone gives delight.

Thirdly, when you have the highest faith in God and the fullest submission to Him, then you are in the best spiritual state. Strive to reach this state.

Fourthly, what do you need most, and what do you desire most? Is it not that God may be all in all in you? But how can this be, unless all human good and evil become nothing in you and mean nothing to you? You would do well to pray this prayer: "O my soul! Rid yourself of everything that is earthly and therefore changeable. While you are waiting for and expecting your Bridegroom, who is the Creator of all beings, let it be your one and only concern that He may find your heart free from all worldly things whenever it pleases Him to visit you."

Be assured of this: sooner or later, we will come to believe that everything in ourselves is evil by nature, and must be entirely given up. We will know for certain that nothing that is human or created can make us better than we are by nature. Therefore, all those spiritual or physical trials that bring us to this conviction are a blessing to us. It is best that we may be driven to seek everything from God with the whole strength of our souls, without the least thought or hope of any other relief. When we have come to this point, we will be made true partakers of the cross of Christ, and from the bottom of our hearts we will be able to say, with Paul, *"God forbid that I should glory, save in the cross of our Lord Jesus Christ, by whom the world is crucified unto me, and I unto the world"* (Gal. 6:14).

Give yourself up to God without reservation. This implies a state of the heart that does nothing of itself, or from its own reason, will, or choice. Rather, it always stands in faith, hope, and absolute dependence upon God, being led by the Spirit into everything that is according to His will. The heart that is yielded to God will seek nothing by its own plans, thoughts, or reason. Instead, it will deal with everything that every day brings as something that comes from God and as something that is to be received and gone through just as Jesus would have done.

I consider this an attainable degree of perfection for all of us. By having Christ and His Spirit always in our view, and nothing else, we will never be left to ourselves, nor will we be without the full guidance of God.

Chapter 16

Regaining Our Original Holiness

In the first part of this final chapter, I want to deal with a topic that has often been the cause of controversy among Christians. The basic question is, How can God be all love and goodness to His creatures, when the Scriptures also say that He hardened the heart of Pharaoh (Exod. 9:12), and that both good and evil come from Him? (See Job 2:10.) *"Therefore hath he mercy on whom he will have mercy, and whom he will he hardeneth"* (Rom. 9:18). God says, *"I form the light, and create darkness"* (Isa. 45:7).

Why do we have so much difficulty reconciling such contrary things that are said about God? We know that He wills life and goodness, and yet evil and death are said to come from Him as well. (See Micah 1:12, for example.) Our difficulties with this arise when with our finite minds we try to consider the operations of God, or when we try to understand the contrary things as if they were said about anyone but God. The operations of God are vastly different from anything that can be done by human beings, and the only relation that His operations

197

have to His creations is the fact that He created them.

This, and this alone, is the working of the Deity in heaven and on earth. Through all eternity, nothing comes from Him or is done by Him in His creatures except an essential manifestation of Himself in them, which restores the glory and perfection of their first existence. He can be nothing else toward the creature besides the same love and goodness that He was at the Creation. Therefore, to the creature who turns from Him, God can be nothing else but the cause of its evil and miserable state. This is why the apostle wrote, *"I had not known sin, but by the law...for without the law sin was dead"* (Rom. 7:7–8). To clarify, sin comes by the law, because where there is no law, there is no transgression.

Now, the divine nature in man is the one great law of God from which all that is good and all that is evil in man has its whole state and nature. The life of a man can have no holiness or goodness in it unless the divine nature within him is the law by which he lives. He can commit no other sin, nor feel any kind of hurt or evil from it, except what comes from resisting or rebelling against the godliness that is in him. Therefore, the good and evil of man are equally from God.

And yet, this could not be so if God's love and goodness could change. What if He did not have only one will and work of love and goodness toward all His creation? The law is immutably righteous, holy, and good (Rom. 7:12), and has only one will and one work toward man, whether he receives good or evil from it. The law is righteous and holy because it never changes its good will and work toward man.

Man, however, changes in his obedience to it. This is how God can truly say these two contrary things, "I cause good" and "I cause evil," without the least contradiction.

On the same basis, it must be said that happiness and misery, life and death, tenderness and hardness of heart, are also from God.

This is the one true key to the state of man before his fall, to his state after his fall, and to the whole nature of his redemption. All three of these states were, in a few words of our Savior, set forth in the clearest and strongest light. John 15:5 describes man's state before the Fall: *"I am the vine, ye are the branches: he that abideth in me, and I in him, the same bringeth forth much fruit."* This was man's first created state of glory and perfection; it consisted of living and abiding in God, communing with Him and having life from Him, just as the branch has its life in and from the vine.

Man's redeemed state is summed up in the following words: *"I am that bread of life...which cometh down from heaven"* (John 6:48, 50); *"he that eateth of this bread shall live for ever"* (v. 58); *"whoso eateth my flesh, and drinketh my blood, hath eternal life...*[he] *dwelleth in me, and I in him"* (vv. 54, 56).

This is our whole redemption; it consists only of having the full life of God, or Christ reborn in us. In this way, our first perfection, our miserable fall, and our blessed redemption have all their glory or all their misery solely from God. God alone is all that is good, and He can be nothing else but good toward the creature who is in Him. Whether angel or man, a created being can only be happy when it has this one

God of goodness truly living and operating in it. Otherwise, it is miserable.

So many things that come under the name of religion are immediately cut off by this! The only thing that brings life, happiness, and glory is the operation of the triune God of love and goodness within us. Death, evil, and misery come when we turn from this essential God of our lives, to something in ourselves or in the people around us. He is deluded who thinks that anything but the body, the blood, and the Spirit of Christ can make him into a new creature and be his atonement, his reconciliation, and his union with God. Only when Christ has made him into a new creature is he that first man whom God created, in whom He can be well pleased. But until then, he is a man whom the cherubim's two-edged flaming sword will not allow to enter into paradise.

The Life of God Revealed in Us

How, then, are we to regain that first birth of Christ? We are to regain it in just the same way as Adam first obtained it. How was that? How did he help promote God's creating power? He did nothing out of his own power. Restoring the first life that we had in God is exactly the same work as God creating us in the beginning. Therefore, we can have no more share of power in the one than in the other. As creatures fallen from God, our only responsibility with regard to our growth in God is not to resist what God is doing toward creating us anew.

All that God is doing toward the new creation of our souls had its beginning before the foundation of the world. Paul said, *"He hath chosen us in him* [Christ] *before the foundation of the world"* (Eph. 1:4). This is the same as saying that God, out of His great mercy, chose to preserve a seed of the Word and Spirit of God in fallen man, and that, through the mediation of a God incarnate, the seed would revive into the fullness of stature in Christ Jesus in which Adam was originally created. This work of God toward a new creation is according to the same essential operation of God in us that first created us in His image and likeness. Therefore, man's sole duty is to yield himself up to it and not resist it.

Who are these people who resist being reborn? They are all who do not deny themselves, take up their crosses daily, and follow Christ. For everything besides this is the flesh warring against the spirit. The natural man resists all the essential operation of God that would recreate him in Christ Jesus. But the natural man is not the only one who resists the work of God. The believer also resists it when he takes anything to be the truth of piety, devotion, or religious worship, except faith, hope, trust, and dependence upon only what the all-creating Word and all-sanctifying Spirit of God work in his soul.

If you want to know how you are to understand this essential operation of the triune, holy Deity in your soul, and why nothing else can be the grace or help of God that brings salvation, consider the following analogy. The light and air of this world are universal powers that are essential to the life of all the creatures of this world. They are essential because the creature cannot see until light makes contact with it, and it cannot live until air is flowing through its lungs. Again, both the light and the air are universal powers, and the creature's light and air must come from these powers.

It is the same with the operation of the triune God in the life of all godly creatures, whether men or angels. The light and the Holy Spirit of God are universal powers, essential to the birth of a godly life in the creature. The rebirth of a divine life in the creature can begin no sooner than the Word and Spirit of God are reborn in the creature. Nor can the divine life survive any longer than it is united with and under the continual operation of that Word and Spirit. Hence, it is truly said that spiritual life and spiritual death, spiritual good and spiritual evil, happiness and misery, are from God, solely because there is no good except in God, and the only operation of God in and to the creature is that of heavenly life, light, love, and goodness.

Man, who was created in the image and likeness of God to be a habitation and manifestation of the triune God of goodness, had turned from his holy state of life in God because of the perverseness of a false will. He was therefore dead to the blessed union and essential operation of God in his soul. However, the goodness of God toward man did not alter, but it stood in the same goodwill toward man as at the first. Toward the whole human race, God willed that every individual might be saved from the state of death and misery into which he had fallen.

God's Providence toward His People

From this unchangeable and unceasing love of God toward man, a wonderful demonstration of providence came forth. God used a variety of means and dispensations—visions, voices, and messages from heaven; laws, prophecies, and promises—all adapted to the different states, conditions, and ages of the fallen world. He did this so that every art of divine wisdom and every act of love could break man away from his earthly delusion and produce in him a sense of his lost glory. Then, man would be capable of experiencing again that blessed, essential operation of Father, Son, and Holy Spirit in his soul, which was the glory of his first creation.

In this demonstration of divine and redeeming providence, God had to deal with poor, blind, earthly creatures who had lost all sense of heavenly things. Even so, the wisdom of God must often humanize itself, as it were, and God must condescend to speak of Himself after the manner of men. He must speak of His eyes, His ears, His hands, His nose, and so on, because the earthly creature, the mere natural man, could in no other way be brought to an awareness of what God is to him.

But now, all these actions of Providence were only for the sake of something higher—the salvation of man and his reunion with God through Christ. Meanwhile, the mystery of God in man, and man in God, still lay hidden. Pentecost was the only thing that took away all the veils and showed the kingdom of God as it was in itself. It set man again under the direct, essential operation of God, which had given birth to a holy Adam in Paradise. Types and shadows ended because the substance of them was found. The cloven tongues of fire put an end to them by opening the spiritual eyes that Adam had closed up, by unstopping the spiritual ears that he had filled with clay, and by making his dumb sons to speak with new tongues.

And what did they say when they spoke with new tongues? They said that all old things are gone, that a new heaven and a new earth are coming forth, and that God Himself has been manifested in the flesh of men, who are now all taught by God Himself. And what are they taught? The same thing that Adam was taught in his first created life in God, namely, that the direct, essential operation of Father, Son, and Holy Spirit is henceforth the birthright of all who become true disciples of Christ. And so, the old creation and the fall of man ended, because God was manifested in the flesh, dying in and for the world and coming again in the Spirit, to be the life and light of all the sons of Adam.